1939-1945
WORLD WAR TWO

AUTHOR

Carlo Cucut was born in Nole (TO) in 1955. He has cultivated a passion for history since he was a boy and over the years has deepened this interest by devoting himself to historical research. He has published articles in the magazines, "History of the 20th Century," "Stories & Battles," "Milites," and "Ritterkreuz." In the publishing field, he has published several volumes for Marvia Editions: "Penne Nere on the Eastern Border. History of the Alpine Regiment "Tagliamento" 1943-1945," winner of the De Cia Prize; "Attilio Viziano. Memories of a War Correspondent"; "Armed Forces of the CSR on the Eastern Front"; "Armed Forces of the CSR on the Western Front"; "Armed Forces of the CSR on the Gothic Line"; "Alpini in the City of Rijeka 1944-1945." For the Gruppo Modellistico Trentino he published "Armed Forces of the CSR 1943-1945. Ground Forces."

Title: **ROMANIAN ARMOURED DIVISIONS** Code.: **WTW-037 ENG** Di Carlo Cucut
ISBN code: 978-88-93278898 First edition October 2022
Text: English Nr. di immagini: 114 Layout: 7X10 Cover & Art Design: Luca S. Cristini

WITNESS TO WAR (SOLDIERSHOP) is a trademark of Luca Cristini Editore, via Orio, 35/4 - 24050 Zanica (BG) ITALY.

WITNESS TO WAR

ROMANIAN ARMOURED DIVISIONS

From the constitution to the end of the Second World War: 1916-1945

PHOTOS & IMAGES FROM WORLD WARTIME ARCHIVES

CARLO CUCUT

BOOKS TO COLLECT

CONTENTS

▲ R-2 tanks with their crews, belonging to Regimentul 1 Care de Luptă, during training in 1940 (from: *Armata română şi evoluţia armei tancuri. Documente (1919-1945)- op. cit. in bibliography*)

ROMANIA: FROM THE WAR AGAINST BULGARIA TO THE END OF THE SECOND WORLD WAR

The Kingdom of Romania (*Regatul României*), which had existed since 13 March 1881 following the Romanian War of Independence, defeated Bulgaria in 1913 during the Second Balkan War and, on the basis of the Treaty of Bucharest of 10 August 1913, obtained the annexation of the Dobruja region and part of the Bulgarian Black Sea coast.

At the outbreak of World War I, the Kingdom of Romania remained neutral for the first two years, but on 27 August 1916, after signing a treaty with the Allies, it took the decision to declare war on Austria-Hungary even though, due to alliances, both Germany and Turkey declared war on Romania. Initially, the Romanian army achieved some victories, conquering Transylvania, but at the beginning of September, General August von Mackensen, commanding an army made up of German, Bulgarian and Turkish troops, counter-attacked and blocked the Romanian advance. From September to December, after receiving numerous reinforcements, the Central Powers' offensive was unleashed, and in a few months they conquered more than half of Romania, including the capital Bucharest, which fell into the hands of the German cavalry on 6 December 1916, and the important oil wells of Ploiești.

The Russian Empire was forced to move hundreds of thousands of soldiers to support the Romanian army and prevent the army under the command of General Erich von Falkenhayn from invading Russia. In the early months of 1917, the Romanian army was reorganised with the help of France and the United Kingdom and managed to organise an offensive with Russian troops in support of General Kerensky's army in May. After achieving important results, due to the failure of the Kerensky offensive, operations were stopped, thus allowing a counter-attack by the army under the command of Field Marshal Mackensen, which was, however, defeated at the Battle of Mărășești, fought between 6 August and 3 September 1917.

The consequence of the fall of the Russian Empire, following the October Revolution, was the signing of the armistice between Germany and Bolshevik Russia in December 1917. This armistice deprived Romania of the support of the Russian army, leaving it in an extremely critical situation. On 9 December 1917, in Focșani, the Kingdom of Romania was forced to conclude an armistice with the Central Powers, followed by the Treaty of Bucharest on 7 May 1918, by which important portions of territory were ceded to the victors.

On 10 November 1918, the Kingdom of Romania decided to denounce the Bucharest Treaty and re-enter the war on the side of the Allies. The renewed Romanian army fought some successful battles in the last weeks of the conflict, regaining several territories ceded as a result of the previous year's defeat. At the end of the conflict, the Kingdom of Romania, an ally of the Entente against the Central Empires, greatly expanded its territory, encompassing Transylvania, Bessarabia and Bukovina. The Treaty of Saint Germain of 1919 ratified the handover of Bukovina to the Kingdom of Romania, while in 1920, the Treaty of Trianon and the Treaty of Paris ratified the possession of Bessarabia and Transylvania.

Thanks to these territorial conquests, the long-desired goal of establishing *România Mare* the 'Greater Romania', a nation state incorporating all Romanian ethnic groups living in the neighbouring nations, was achieved. However, as these newly conquered territories also included large Hungarian, German, Bulgarian, Ukrainian and Russian minorities, there were numerous conflicts with the neighbouring nations, which even resulted in violent conflicts, such as the Hungarian-Romanian War and the Tatar insurrection.

In the 1920s and 1930s, the Kingdom of Romania was plagued by numerous political crises, which led to the formation of as many as 25 different governments, without remedying the difficulties the country was facing. In this political instability, the increased power of the military emerged, which materialised with the appointment of General Ion Antonescu as Prime Minister on 4 September 1940. When World War II broke out, the Kingdom of Romania declared its neutrality, but allowed the fleeing Polish government to transit and maintained relations with the western powers.

As provided for in the articles of the Molotov-Ribbentrop Pact concerning the division of European territories, the Soviet Union sent an ultimatum to Romania on 26 June 1940, which was followed by the occupation of Bessarabia, Northern Bukovina and the Herța Territory between 28 June and 4 July 1940. Since the Kingdom of Romania did not resist the Soviet Union, Hungary and Bulgaria also took the opportunity to regain possession of the territories ceded in 1918. With the Second Vienna Arbitration of 30 August 1940, through the mediation of Germany and Italy, Northern Transylvania was ceded to Hungary, while with the Treaty of Craiova of 7 September 1940, again through German-Italian mediation, Southern Dobruja returned to Bulgaria. As a result of these territorial cessions, the Kingdom of Romania lost almost half of its territory.

On 6 September 1940, General Antonescu forced King Carol II to abdicate in favour of his son Michael I and proclaimed himself *Conducător* (Duce), assuming full powers and moving ever closer to Hitler's Germany, leaving the monarchy with a purely formal task.

With the promise to recover Bessarabia, Bukovina, some territories in Ukraine and to review the situation in Transylvania, Germany convinced the Kingdom of Romania to join the Tripartite Pact on 23 November 1940. In 1941 it joined Germany in the invasion of Russia (Operation Barbarossa), participating with a military contingent second in size only to that of Germany. After the victory at Stalingrad, the Red Army began the overwhelming advance that brought it to the borders of the Kingdom of Romania in the summer of 1944.

Taking note of the situation, King Michael I, in a coup supported by the military and political parties, dismissed Antonescu on 23 August 1944 and signed the armistice with the Allies. The Romanian army then began fighting against the former German ally, flanking the Red Army units, fighting with some units, after the liberation of Romania, in Hungary, Czechoslovakia and Austria until the end of the world conflict in May 1945.

After the war, following the Paris Peace Conference, approximately one fifth of the surface area of the Kingdom of Romania was ceded to the Soviet Union and Bulgaria. King Michael I, after being decorated with the USSR Victory Medal, was forced to abdicate on 30 December 1947, replaced by a republic ruled by the Romanian Communist Party. In 1948 the monarchy was officially abolished and the Constitution of the Romanian People's Republic was launched.

ROMANIAN ARMOURED UNITS

From 1916 to 1934

The *Forțele Terestre Române* (Romanian Land Forces) entered the First World War with a numerically substantial but materially weak staff, there were no armoured cars and tanks, furthermore, vehicles were present in an insignificant number, given the size of the army, most transport was still animal-drawn. This situation reflected the country's predominantly agricultural economy, with a backward industrial sector where, apart from the mining industry in the Ploiesti area, there were very few mechanical and metallurgical companies.

The consequence of these industrial shortcomings was that, both before and throughout the conflict, only two armoured cars of national design were built in Romania. At the workshops of the *Căile Ferate Române-CFR* in 1915, an armoured car was designed and built using the chassis of a truck under repair armed with a machine gun. During the war, the workshops were moved to Iași, where a second, larger armoured car was built, armed with a machine gun and a 57 mm Hotchkiss cannon modified for anti-aircraft firing with the system invented by officer Ștefan Burileanu.

The first armoured unit of the Romanian army was formed in 1916, equipped with four combat vehicles, two Peugeots and two Renaults, armed with 8 mm French Chatellerault machine guns, and was called *Grupul de automitraliere*. In November 1916, after receiving two more armoured cars, the unit changed its name to *Grup de autoblindate* (Armoured Group).

The *Grup de autoblindate* participated in operations on the Soveja road and in the Grozești gorge, as part of the offensive developed by the Second Army in July 1917. In the course of 1917, several 'Austin' and 'Austin-Putilov' armoured cars were captured from Russian deserters and were immediately used by the Romanians during the fighting in the following years.

Most of the few dozen[1] armoured cars used during the conflict were of Russian origin, built on the basis of different chassis: Austin-Putilov, Garford-Putilov, Peugeot, Izhorski-Fiat, vehicles that were in any case worn out, many damaged and in need of constant maintenance.

At the end of the conflict, the Command of the *Forțele Terestre Române realised* the potential expressed by the new armoured and armoured vehicles and decided in the spring of 1919 to proceed with the purchase of tanks and to set up armoured units.

Between the end of 1918 and the beginning of 1919, a new armoured car called *Automobil blindat M1919* entered service. It was built in Romania on the basis of a Renault truck chassis armoured with 6- and 8-mm-thick sheet metal, equipped with a hexagonal rotating turret armed with a machine gun. Together with a number of armoured cars already in service, it was used during the Hungarian-Romanian War of July/August 1919, during which a Romfell armoured car was also captured and then used for a few years.

With the armoured cars in service, two companies were established in the course of 1919, although the variety and precarious condition of the vehicles, aggravated by the lack of spare parts and the shortage of specialised technical personnel for repairs, immediately affected the companies' operations.

Taking note of the difficulties encountered, the decision was made to found a school dedicated to the training of armoured troops and to establish the first armoured units. Since neither the training and professional skills nor the means and equipment were available to begin the establishment of

---

1 Some sources cite a total of 34 armoured cars that entered service, but without indicating the numbers of the different makes and their state of efficiency.

what was planned, it was decided to turn to the most willing and present ally at the time: France. As a first act, in April 1919, Royal Decree No. 1527 was issued, sanctioning the establishment of the Şcolii *de Care de Asalt* (Assault School), assigned to the command of Colonel Pandele Predescu. While an ad hoc commission was sent to France on 7 June 1919, under the command of Colonel Traian Pascal, to establish contacts with tank manufacturers and visit the Armoured Troops Training Schools, meetings with the French delegation were intensified in Romania, who agreed to make available, as of 1 July 1919, the 303[a] Assault Company[2], consisting of 6 officers, 108 soldiers, 19 tanks and 12 cars, for the new Şcolii *de Care de Asalt,* although, this allocation was subject to change in the event of critical situations arising in areas of French influence.

On 9 July, the French informed General Radu R. Rosetti that, as stipulated in the clauses of the agreement signed on 1 July, they would reduce the personnel and means of the 303[a] Assault Company assigned to training at the Şcolii *de Care de Asalt due to* unforeseen needs.

The School was initially supposed to be established at the military garrison in Mihai Bravu, but following checks carried out at the site, it was decided to start the courses in Giurgiu and at the same time provide logistical accommodation in the Mihai Bravu area.

On 21 July 1919 in Giurgiu, in the barracks of the 5th Infantry Regiment *"Vlaşca", the* activity of the Şcolii *de Care de Asalt officially* began, initiating the first cycle of training for tank personnel, which lasted from 21 July to 10 September 1919, during which the following were trained: 16 officers, 2 reserve officers, 5 military squad leaders and 4 drivers. The Romanian tank drivers were specifically trained on:

- Technical instruction of 'Renault' FT-17 light wagon
- FT-17 'Renault' light tank tactical instruction on driving, arming and firing

Meanwhile, on 16 July, the commission under the orders of Colonel Pascal had reported back home that it had agreed to the transfer to Romania of 76 Renault FT17 tanks[3], 48 armed with the Puteaux SA 18 calibre 37 mm cannon and the remaining 28 with the Hotchkiss Mle 1914 8 mm calibre machine gun, as well as equipment and spare parts. It was also planned to supply at least three TFS command tanks with radio equipment, but these were not delivered. The tanks were allocated to the new armoured division.

In application of Order No. 1401 issued by the General Secretariat of the Ministry of War, on 1 August 1919, the first Romanian armoured unit was officially constituted: the *Batalionul 1 Care de Luptă. This* was the beginning of the history of the *Forţele Terestre Române* armoured units.

Installed at the Şcolii *de Care de Asalt,* with which it shared its headquarters and commander, the *Batalionul 1 Care de Luptă* was placed under the 3[a] Artillery Directorate.

The formation of the battalion, consisting of four companies, repair workshop and mobile workshop, was completed on 1 October, with a staff of 25 officers and 376 non-commissioned officers, graduates and soldiers.

As the works on the infrastructure and the premises of the garrison in Mihai Bravu had been completed in October, the transfer of the Şcolii *de Care de Asalt* to the new premises took place on 28 October 1919, where the Romanian instructors, trained in Giurgiu, started their activity in favour of the recruits. However, even the new headquarters in Mihai Bravu did not meet the needs related to the formation of an armoured unit, so Colonel Predescu prepared an accurate technical report that was sent to the Minister of War, who intervened by approving the transfer of *Batalionul 1 Care de Luptă* to Târgovişte.

---

2 According to another source, the company in charge of training the Romanians was the 302nd Assault Company, deriving from the 303rd Assault Company deployed at Reni in Bessarabia.

3 Some sources put the number of Renault FT-17 tanks purchased at 72, 45 armed with cannon and 27 with machine guns.

▲ The first armoured car built in Romania at the *Căile Ferate Române-CFR* in 1915 *(https://en.wikipedia.org/wiki/ File:1915_-_Automobil_blindat.jpg)*

▼ Automobil blindat M1919 in Budapest during the brief war between Romania and Hungary in July/August 1919 *(https://wofmd.com/2019/02/12/automobil-blindat-m1919/)*

In April 1920, the delivery of the tanks and logistics equipment was completed, these also included 32 French tractors for towing the tanks and 7 Fiat light trucks. All the material was delivered to Giurgiu, where a commission, composed of Colonel Predescu, Major Negrescu and Captains Nicolau and Vâlveanu, checked the quality and efficiency of the material to be subsequently assigned to the divisions.

By High Royal Decree No. 5488 issued on 25.12.1920, in force since 1 January 1921, the *Regimentul Carelor de Luptă* (Tank Regiment) was established. The *Batalionul 1 Care de Luptă, the armoured* trains, the armoured car companies and the machine gun company, with a total staff of 26 officers and 764 soldiers, were brought into the new structure. This structure immediately highlighted the problems arising from the operational differences of the vehicles in service and the tactics in use.

In 1922, the armoured trains were handed over to the anti-aircraft artillery regiment, and on 1 April the *Care de Luptă Regiment* assumed the following structure:

- Headquarters
- Deposit
- Repair workshop
- *Batalionul 1 Care de Luptă* (3 Tank Companies and 1 Transport Company)
- Machine gun/armoured car battalion (2 machine gun companies and 1 armoured car company)

In the summer of 1924, the General Staff of the *Forțele Terestre Române* began to consider the establishment of a second tank battalion. In 1925, the regiment underwent a new reorganisation, as the machine gun/armoured car battalion was transferred to the Cavalry Training Centre in Sibiu.

During 1926, the *Regimentul Carelor de Luptă*, following yet another reorganisation and the establishment of the second tank battalion, took on the following structure:

- Headquarters
- *Batalionul 1 Care de Luptă*
- *Batalionul 2 Care de Luptă*
- Armoured car company
- Repair workshop

with a total staff of 34 officers, 385 non-commissioned officers, graduates and soldiers, and 22 civilians.

▲ The Armoured Squadron of the Cavalry Training Centre in Sibiu in 1927, the armoured car on the left is an Austin while the one on the right is a Renault *(www.resboiu.ro/95-de-ani-de-la-infiintarea-armei-tancurilor)*

▲ Romanian armoured cars belonging to the *Grup de autoblindate* in Bazau in the winter of 1916 *(www.iwm.org.uk/collections/item/object/205320856)*

The tank battalions consisted of three companies: two tank companies and one transport company. The tank companies were each equipped with 19 Renault FT-17 tanks, organised into three platoons of five tanks, three of which were armed with cannon and two with machine guns. The total number of tanks in service amounted to 76 FT-1917 tanks. In March 1928, the Education Office was also established within the Regiment, a structure specialised in planning and coordinating training activities, while in 1929, the war flag was solemnly handed over.

Once the structure of the *Regimentul Carelor de Luptă* had been consolidated, the training of the crews and the training activities of the units continued, however, highlighting the increasing difficulties of the available means, which were worn out and in need of continuous and thorough maintenance. The limited availability of operational means reached its peak in 1930, when only 34 tanks and armoured cars were still operational, although they were very often in poor condition.

The industrial backwardness of Romania, the lack of metallurgical and mechanical industries, the poor mechanisation in general and of the Army in particular, with an essentially agricultural economy and with the transport sector still largely centred on animal and railway towing, came to the surface once again, as had already happened in the First World War. Not only was the Army poorly motorised and mechanised, but repairing vehicles in service was also problematic, given the absence of domestic motor industries capable of producing parts and training qualified technicians. The only automotive company in the country was Ford Romania, which assembled vehicles by importing parts from abroad.

But it was not only the production of vehicles that was inadequate for the needs of the *Forţele Terestre Române*, the repair sector of the vehicles in service was also lacking. Apart from the army repair shop, only a few workshops belonging to the Leonid company were present and capable of carrying out repairs and maintenance on operational vehicles.

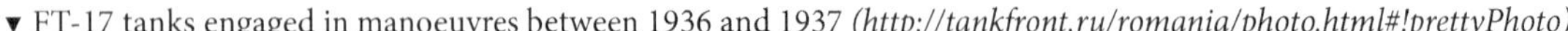

▲ Officers and tank drivers around an FT-17 tank near the Tisza River in the early 1920s *(http://tankfront.ru/romania/photo.html#!prettyPhoto)*

▼ FT-17 tanks engaged in manoeuvres between 1936 and 1937 *(http://tankfront.ru/romania/photo.html#!prettyPhoto)*

Two factors heavily influenced the growth of the Romanian armoured forces: the training carried out by the French, which brought to the Romanians their doctrine, aimed more at infantry support than at armoured combat, and the industrial backwardness that prevented them from producing viable armoured and armoured vehicles.

The integral application of French doctrine meant that Romanian tank units were trained to support the infantry, divided into small units operating under the command of the infantry or artillery units to which they were assigned in support. Numerous young officers sought to learn more about the operational doctrines and organisation of armoured troops from other nations, the Soviet Union, Italy, Great Britain and later Germany, producing studies and documentation comparing the different operational doctrines and organisation of the units. Despite this doctrinal turmoil, however, no changes were made, the *Regimentul Carelor de Luptă* remained unchanged with the tasks stipulated by the French doctrine.

The industrial backwardness officially emerged following an in-depth inspection by the Romanian General Staff in 1934, which ruled that it was impossible to produce armoured vehicles independently in Romania, thus forcing the *Forțele Terestre Române* to have to resort to foreign companies to purchase all the vehicles needed for the renewal of the combat line.

The realisation of the deficient operational situation of the *Regimentul Carelor de Luptă, the* difficulties related to industrial backwardness, the improvement of the country's economic conditions, the European political situation, finally led the General Staff of the *Forțele Terestre Române* to draw up a plan to strengthen the armoured forces.

▲ An FT-17 tank engaged in an infantry exercise in the late 1930s *(http://tankfront.ru/romania/photo.html#!prettyPhoto)*

▲ FT-17 tanks during winter manoeuvres in the late 1920s.

▼ Romanian and French officers, with some tank men in fatigue uniforms, pose with two Renault FT-17s in front of the Şcolii *de Care de Asalt* in Giurgiu in August 1919.

Rearmament: 1935 to 1940

The oil exports[4] enabled a marked improvement in Romania's economic situation in the 1930s, allowing the approval in 1935 of an ambitious 10-year rearmament programme for the *Forțele Terestre Române. The* main objective of the plan was to rearm the army by standardising its weapons, improve and expand the motorisation and mechanisation of the infantry and artillery. The plan also included the upgrading of armoured units. It should be emphasised that the modernisation programme was realistic and was adhered to on schedule, with the objectives being achieved every year until its expiry date.

Given the absence of domestic companies capable of meeting the requirements of the rearmament plan, it was forced to turn to foreign companies. To replace the outdated and ultra-worn Renault FT-17s in service, Romanian procurement officers turned to the leading European armoured vehicle companies: Vickers, Renault, Polish Ursus, ČKD and Škoda.

After evaluating numerous vehicles, the Czechoslovak companies ČKD (Českomoravská Kolben-Daněk) and Škoda were asked on 8 January 1936 to submit an offer for the supply of tanks for the Romanian Army. On 14 August 1936, preliminary contracts were signed in Prague, with very strict conditions applied, for the supply of 35 Praga AH-IV light tanks by the ČKD company and 126 LT-35 light tanks by the Škoda company.

The Praga AH-IV was a light tank weighing 3.5 tons, equipped with 12 mm thick armour, armed with a ZB-37 heavy machine gun and a ZB-30 light machine gun both in 7.92 mm calibre in a rotating turret, with a 60 hp Praga RHR V6 engine[5] and an improved Praga-Wilson transmission. The wagon upon its entry into service in the *Forțele Terestre Române was* named R-1, while the designation for the ČKD was AH-IV-R. Deliveries of the R-1 began in 1937 and were completed in mid-1938. On 22 February 1939 an agreement was signed with the ČKD for the licensed production of a further 380 R-1 wagons by the Romanian company Malaxa, the wagons produced in Romania would be designated R-1-a. Malaxa only built one prototype, because, following the experiences of the light tanks during the war in Poland, the General Staff decided not to purchase any more light tanks, which were considered unsuitable for combat.

R-1 tanks were given to cavalry brigades 5, 6 and 8, which each received six R-1 tanks, while brigades 1, 7 and 9 received four. The Cavalry Training Centre in Sibiu was also given the R-1 tank until 1943. The Lehký Tank vzor 35 - LT vz. 35, the official factory designation was Š-II-a, was a light tank built by Škoda at the request of the Czechoslovak Army, deliveries of which began in July 1936. It was armed with a 37 mm cannon, armour ranging from 16 mm to 25 mm and a 118 hp Škoda T-11/0 engine that allowed it to reach a speed of 35 km/h. The Romanian tanks had armour that was less thick in places than the original vehicle and a modified turret; they were designated R-2 while the Škoda was named Š-IIa-R.

The development of the R-2 was plagued by numerous problems, mainly related to the fact that the LT vz. 35 was a new vehicle, plagued by numerous 'teething' problems that Škoda solved in itinere, but which in 1937 still showed rather poor reliability. In addition, various Romanian officials involved in the programme made numerous requests for modifications, sometimes illogical, which caused considerable delays in the development of the prototype. Two versions were thus produced: the standard R-2 tank with mild steel plates and the R-2c tank with case-hardened steel plates[6].

---

4 The main extraction facilities were located in Ploiești.
5 Some sources claim that in Romania the wagons had their engines depowered to around 50 hp to further improve their durability.
6 One half R-2 tank and the other half R-2a. The two tanks could be distinguished by the different shape of the rear turret and in the rear armouring of the hull.

▲ Officers and tank crew around an FT-17 tank in 1939 *(http://tankfront.ru/romania/photo.html#!prettyPhoto)*

▲ The R-1 light wagon prototype undergoing trials at the ČKD factory *(https://warspot.net/190-little-tank-great-success)*

▼ FT-17 tanks belonging to the *Batalionul Carelor de Lupta FT in* Odessa in April 1942 *(https://forums.tripwireinteractive. com/index.php?)*

▲ Interior of an R-1 light wagon under construction *(https://thereaderwiki.com/en/R-1_tank)*

As deliveries were delayed and Romania wanted to start training on the new tanks, Czechoslovakia loaned 15 LT-35 tanks in May 1937. As well as being used to start training, these 15 LT-35s participated in the parade at the end of July 1938 in Bucharest, and then returned to Škoda where they were brought up to R-2 tank standard.

The delivery of the 126 R-2 tanks was not completed until February 1939, when the last 32 tanks arrived in Romania to complete the order signed in 1936, they were all assigned to *Regimentul 1 Carelor de Luptă*[7].

As far as the supply of armoured vehicles was concerned, Romania not only turned to Czechoslovakia, but also continued its cooperation with France by signing an agreement in December 1937 to build 200 Renault R35 tanks under licence. However, due to obvious industrial shortages, the agreement could not be finalised and the R35 tanks were purchased directly. Due to the needs of the French army, and the deliveries already under way to Yugoslavia, Poland and Turkey, the delivery of the wagons destined for Romania was considerably delayed. By the end of 1939, only 41 R35s had been delivered out of the 200 ordered. Following the occupation of France by the Germans, the order was cancelled and so only a total of 41 new R35s entered service.

The R35s in Romania had the original 7.5 mm Chatellerault machine gun replaced with the Czechoslovak 7.22 mm ZB machine gun and, in the following years, changes were also made to the suspension and the replacement of the bogie tyred wheels with metal ones[8].

---

7 New Name of the *Regimentul Carelor de Luptă*.
8 This tank was disliked by Romanian tank drivers because it was well-armoured but very slow, unreliable and without a radio.

▲ An R-1 light tank during training in 1939 *(http://tankfront.ru/romania/photo.html#!prettyPhoto)*

Following the Polish Campaign, which broke out on 3 September 1939, part of the 305th Polish Battalion crossed into Romania at the end of September, handing over a total of 34 R35 tanks belonging to the unit to the Romanian armed forces. According to the agreement between the Romanian and Polish authorities, the vehicles were incorporated into the *Forțele Terestre Române* while the personnel were embarked on ships that reached the United Kingdom. Thanks to this unexpected delivery, the total number of Renault R35 tanks in service in the Romanian army at the end of 1939 was 75 vehicles. All R35 tanks, designated Care de Lupta Tip R-35, were delivered to *Regimentul 2 Care de Luptă*, established on 1 November 1939.

In addition to the R35 tanks, a dozen Renault UE Chenillettes, a light tracked armoured vehicle designed to tow the Schneider 47 mm anti-tank gun, were purchased from France in 1937. Intending to create a domestic industry capable of producing armoured vehicles, the Romanian Ministry of Defence acquired a licence for the local production of 300 Chenillettes in 1937. The licence was acquired by the Malaxa Company of Bucharest and the vehicle was designated Șenileta Malaxa Tipul UE. With the exception of the engine, gearbox and instrument panel, all other vehicle components were produced by Malaxa, with production starting in the second half of 1939 and ending in March 1941, due to the interruption of supplies from the French side following the defeat against the Germans, for a total of 126 vehicles. In 1941, some 50 French Renault UE Chenillettes, captured by the Germans in France, were delivered to Romania by Germany. The total number of vehicles in service in the *Forțele Terestre Române* at the beginning of Operation Barbarossa thus amounted to 178 vehicles, of which 126 Șenileta Malaxa Tipul UE and 52 Renault.

▲ An R-1 light wagon engaged in evaluation tests preparatory to the purchase of the vehicle in 1935.

Between 1936 and 1937, *Regimentul 1 Care de Luptă,* thanks to the new tanks already delivered or being delivered, was organised into three battalions. In relation to military equipment, the battalions were named as follows: 1st Battalion "Renault", 2nd Battalion "R2" and 3rd Battalion" R2".

Noting France's difficulties in meeting R35 wagon deliveries, Romania again turned to Czechoslovakia in search of a medium-sized wagon suitable for the required characteristics. A Romanian delegation visited ČKD, where they were shown the new AH-IV-S light tank, the improved TNH-S and the V-8-H, and then Škoda, where they could see the Š-ID and Š-Ij light self-propelled guns and the Š-Iic medium tank. The Romanian delegation was particularly interested in the R-2a light tank[9] and the V-8-H and T-21 medium tanks[10]. In May 1939, the tanks were tested in the Suditi polygon, which they passed easily. Romania then ordered 216 T-21 medium tanks from Škoda and 395 TNHPS light tanks from ČKD[11], but the Germans intervened and blocked the export of the ordered tanks.

The improvement of vehicles in the *Forțele Terestre Române* did not only take place through purchases, but during 1939 through the requisitioning of tanks and armoured cars, in service in Czechoslovakia and Poland[12], which had entered Romania as a result of the German occupations. The first vehicles requisitioned were 3 OA vz.27 armoured cars, 9 OA vz.30 and 1 LT-35 tank belonging

9 This was the R-2 tank equipped with an upgraded engine, increased armouring and a radio system.
10 Czechoslovakia ceded the production licence of the T21 to Hungary and the tank was produced by the Hungarian industry under the name Turán I.
11 This was the LT vz 38 tank, for the Germans Panzerkampfwagen 38(t).
12 See section on the Renault R-35 wagon.

to the Czechoslovak 7th Tank Battalion, which crossed the Romanian borders to avoid surrendering their vehicles to the Germans in March 1939. The armoured cars OA vz.27 and OA vz.30 were used for internal security activities, at least 2 OA vz.27 were destroyed during the bombing raids on Ploieşti during the summer of 1944, while the OA vz.30 seems to have been in service with Marshal Antonescu's bodyguard[13], at least 3 were destroyed during the bombing raids on Ploieşti.

While the entry into service of the new tanks was proceeding, some 60[14] Renault FT-17 tanks (named FT17) remained in service at the end of 1938, with which an autonomous battalion, the *Batalionul Carelor de Lupta FT,* was established with the task of providing security for the oil installations. On 1 September 1939, the *Centrului de instructie motomecanizat* (Motorised Training Centre)[15] was established in Târgovişte, with the task of training future tank drivers, and on 1 November the *Regimentul 2 Carelor de Luptă* was officially established in Târgu Mureş.

▲ An R-2 tank parades in Bucharest during the parade to conquer the city of Odessa in October 1941, you can distinctly see the "Michael I Cross" in the three colors white-yellow-red painted on the open hood doors *(http://tankfront.ru/romania/photo.html#!prettyPhoto)*

---

13 This was the Batalionul de gardă al mareşalului Antonescu, later expanded into Regimentul de gardă al Conducătorului Statului.
14 In reality, only 20 FT17 tanks were operational.
15 All FT wagons in service were assigned to the Motorised Training Centre.

An R-1 light tank belonging to a Cavalry Division during a ceremony inside a barracks *(http://tankfront.ru/romania/ photo.html#!prettyPhoto)*

▼ The 31ˢᵗ R-1 light tank ready for delivery, note the coat of arms of Carol II painted on the turret *(https://thereaderwiki. com/en/R-1_tank)*

▲ Bucharest parade of Şenileta Malaxa Tipul UE with the Schneider 47 light AT gun in tow in 1940 (*www.facebook.com/Count-High-School-Girls-und-Panzer-1548083418836988*)

▼ A Şenileta Malaxa Tipul UE during a parade in 1940 (*www.cartula.ro/forum/topic/15383-malaxa-renault-ue-2-al-trei-lea-deget-dintr-un-pumn-de-fier/*)

▲ A Şenileta Malaxa Tipul UE parades in Chişinău after the capture of the city (*www.cartula.ro/forum/topic/15383-malaxa-renault-ue-2-al-treilea-deget-dintr-un-pumn-de-fier/*)

▼ R-2 tanks ready for delivery to Romania at the Škoda factory in February 1939 (*https://thereaderwiki.com/en/Panzer_35(t)#Variants*)

▲ R-35 tanks belonging to *Regimentul 2 Care de Luptă* in barracks in Bucharest in 1940 *(from: Armata română şi evoluţia armei tancuri. Documente (1919-1945)- op. cit. in bibliography)*

▼ R-35 tanks belonging to *Regimentul 2 Care de Luptă in* barracks in Bucharest in 1940 (*www.worldwar2.ro/media/?article=366)*

▲ Column of Czechoslovak armoured cars belonging to the 3ᵃ company, the second armoured car is an OA27 with registration number 13,349 and is one of the three OA vz. 27 that were reused by the Romanians, following internment and confiscation, after crossing the border in 1939 *(https://www.valka.cz/OA-vz-27-13-349-t54508)*

▼ The Czechoslovak armoured car OA vz. 30 with the number plate 13387 was one of the nine OA vz. 30 that between 16 and 17 March 1939 were interned and reused by the Romanians after Czechoslovakia was invaded by the Germans (https://www.valka.cz/CZK-OA-vz-30-t10104)

Romania's accession to the Tripartite Pact and German military influence 1940 - 1941

In January 1940, the *Motorized Brigade 1* was formed in Târgoviște, consisting of the two battle tank regiments, with *Regimentul 1 Carelor de Luptă* armed with the 126 R-2 light tanks and *Regimentul 2 Carelor de Luptă* with the 75 R-35s. The evaluations of the Polish Campaign were undoubtedly the basis for the establishment of the Motorised Brigade, although from a technical point of view, the shortcomings related to the type of tanks present and the organisation of the new formation were certainly an obstacle to the Brigade's operability. But even more than the technical aspect, it was the operational doctrine, still tied to the French concept of using tanks to support infantry, that placed limits on the achievement of those results obtained by German troops in Poland.

On 2 July 1940, the first combat of the Romanian armoured units took place in Giurgiulesti, near the bridge over the river Prut, during the evacuation of Bessarabia following the occupation by the Soviet Union. The 5ᵃ company belonging to the 2ⁿᵈ battalion of the *Regimentul 1 Carelor de Luptă,* commanded by Captain Popescu, and a column of about 70 Soviet armoured and armoured vehicles clashed. The three platoons equipped with R-2 tanks opened fire with armour-piercing shells when the Soviet tanks arrived 300 metres away, firing about 80 shells, destroying four enemy tanks. It should be noted that the Soviet tanks returned fire, however, using only explosive shells without causing any damage to the Romanian tanks.

As the dark mists of war were gathering over Europe with increasing speed, Romania drew ever closer politically to Nazi Germany. On 12 October 1940, following the ratification of the agreement signed by the Romanian government with the Foreign Minister of the Third Reich, a German Military Mission arrived in Romania, with the task of training the *Forțele Terestre Române* according to German military doctrine. The German instructors' tasks also included training the Romanians to carry out operations with complex armoured units and blitzkrieg. Changing the mentality of the

▲ **Șenileta** Malaxa Tipul UE with the Schneider 47 light AT gun in tow parading in Bucharest in 1939 (*www.pressreader. com/uk/history-of-war/20201001/282449941461643*)

high commands about the use of armoured units, applying German doctrine, was a challenging task for the Germans, too strong was the resistance of the infantry commanders to deprive themselves of tank support, as they had been taught for decades by applying French doctrine!

Meanwhile, on 23 November 1940, Romania joined the Tripartite Pact, binding its political future to Germany, Italy and Japan.

On 17 April 1941, *the motorized Brigade 1* was transformed into the *Divizia 1 Blindată* (1ª Armoured Division) thanks to the assistance of German instructors and the intensive training carried out. The organisational structure of the Division included the following departments:

- Headquarters
- 101st Exploring Group
- Road Platoon
- Military police platoon
- Batalionul 1 Specialități Motomecanizat
- Batalionul 1 Geniu Motorizat
- *Regimentul 1 Care de Luptă*
- *Regimentul 2 Care de Luptă*
- *Regimentul 3 'Vânători Moto'*
- *Regimentul 4 'Vânători Moto'*
- *Regimentul 1 Artilerie Motorizat*
- Divisional services

It was therefore a very heavy division with a strength of four regiments, with the tank regiments consisting of two battalions each of three tank companies and a maintenance company, the two 'Vânători Moto' (motorised hunters) regiments also consisting of two battalions each of three infantry companies and a machine gun company, a motorised artillery regiment with a 75 mm gun group, a 100 mm howitzer group, a 105 mm gun group, as well as a motorised scout group and various service units.

▲ Group of Şenileta Malaxa Tipul UE captured by the Soviets during the fighting at Stalingrad (http://tankfront.ru/romania/photo.html#!prettyPhoto)

During the training in mass deployment tactics of the armoured units, the differences in the speed and operational characteristics of the R-2 tanks compared to the R-35s became apparent, differences that made a unified deployment of the two regiments extremely difficult. Therefore, the decision was taken to eliminate the R-35 tank *Regimentul 2 Care de Luptă* from *Divizia 1 Blindată,* which became an autonomous tank regiment.

Despite being considered a strong armoured unit on paper, in reality there were numerous deficiencies in both combat and support vehicles. There were only 109 R-2 tanks in service in June 1941, there was a shortage of spare parts and the repair workshops had little equipment to carry out repairs in the field, with the result that most of the tanks to be repaired had to be transported to the Arsenal with a long lead time before they could be re-equipped, there was a lack of radio operators and cooperation between the various arms was considered by the Germans to be insufficient, it was only at a fair level at platoon level. Because of these shortcomings, the Germans considered *Divizia 1 Blindată to* be a Reinforced Regiment, whereas the Soviets considered it to be a Brigade.

On the date of Romania's entry into the war, 22 June 1941, *Divizia 1 Blindată* had the following organisation:

- Headquarters
- Exploring Group
- Road Platoon
- Military police platoon
- Motorised Specialist Battalion

▲ The crew of an R-2 tank, belonging to *Regimentul 1 Care de Luptă,* pose with some officers in 1941 (*https://es-la.facebook.com/1438185513093766/posts/historia-militarrumania-tanques-ligeros-r1-r2tanque-ligero*)

- Motorbike Companion
    - 1^a and 2^a Anti-Aircraft Company
    - 1^a and 2^a Anti-tank company
- Battalion 1 Motorised Engineers
- Pioneer Company
- 101^a Transmission Company
- Bridge Materials Company
- *Regimentul 1 Care de Luptă*
    - Headquarters
    - Command Company
    - Batalion 1.Care de Lupta
    - Batalion 2.Care de Lupta
- *Regimentul 3./4.Vanatori Motorizate*[16]
    - Headquarters
    - Command Company
    - Batalion 1.Vanatori Motorizate / Regimentul 3.Vanatori Motorizate
    - Batalion 2.Vanatori Motorizate / Regimentul 4.Vanatori Motorizate
- *Regiment 1.Artilerie Motorizate*
    - Headquarters
    - Transmission Platoon
    - Antiaircraft Platoon
- Divizion 1.Artilerie - 3 Batteries
- Divizion 2.Artilerie - 3 Batterie
- Divizion 3.Artilerie - 3 Batteries
- Divisional services

Regimentul 1 Care de Luptă consisted of two tank battalions, each with 3 tank companies, consisting of 5 platoons each with 3 R-2s, and a repair company, with a total of 109 R-2s in service.

Regimentul 2 Care de Luptă consisted of two tank battalions, each with 3 tank companies, consisting of 3 platoons each with 3 R-35s, and a repair company, with a total of 75 R-35s in service. Having become autonomous, the Regiment was transferred to the Headquarters of the 4th Army and assigned to the 3rd Army Corps during the campaign to recapture Bessarabia and Northern Bukovina and the siege of Odessa.

---

16 The Regimentul 3./4.Vanatori Motorizate was a Regiment of Motorised Hunters composed of two battalions belonging one to the 3rd and one to the 4th Regimentul Vanatori Motorizate, the remaining two battalions of the regiments remained in their depot in Romania, finishing their motorisation and training.

▲ An R-2 tank taken from ¾ rear where one can see the detail that distinguishes it from the LT vz. 35, the rear of the turret consists of two riveted plates, while that of the LT vz. 35 is in a single sheet *(www.facebook.com/Count-High-School-Girls-und-Panzer-1548083418836988)*

▼ Infantrymen belonging to *Regimentul 2 Care de Luptă* pose on an R-35 tank in the Târgovişte barracks in 1939 *(https://relicsandmilitaria.ro/romanian-army-motorized-tank-unit-officer-parade-belt-buckle/)*

▲ German troops overtake trucks with troops and a Romanian R-2 tank on the Orhei - Chisinau road on 15 July 1941
(http://tankfront.ru/romania/photo.html#!prettyPhoto)

22 June 1941 - Romania enters the war

On Sunday 22 June 1941, Operation Barbarossa, the name given to the invasion of the Soviet Union by Germany and some Axis allied nations, began. The early stages of the conflict also affected the Romanian front, although it mainly involved artillery exchanges, scouting runs by both sides and numerous actions by the air forces on both sides and on the border towns.

The general offensive on the Prut River Front, Operation München - Operaţiunea München, was launched on 2 July, involving the *Divizia 1 Blindată*. Subordinated to the 11th[a] German Army, under the command of Brigadier General Ion Sion, the *Divizia 1 Blindată* started its military operations on 3rd July 1941, when it crossed the Prut by crossing the Ţefăneşti Bridge, heading towards Moghilău cooperating with German units belonging to the 11th Army Corps and the Romanian Cavalry Corps. He then contributed, together with the units of the 22[a] and 76[a] German Infantry Division, to the conquest of Brânzeni on the 4th of July and chased the retreating Soviet troops. The first clash between Romanian and Soviet tanks of World War II was fought in Brânzeni, when a platoon of R-2 tanks was attacked by a dozen Soviet tanks. In the clash, two T-28s and an R-2 were destroyed. On 8 July it reached the Dnestr River, then headed towards Soroca, in pursuit of the Soviet 176[a] Rifle Division, then Bălţi, where on 12 July it came under the orders of the German 54th Army Corps, deploying in support of the Romanian 4[a] Army.

On 14 July, *Divizia 1 Blindată went on the* attack against the strong Soviet defences set up to defend the Corneşti massif, managing to break through the defensive lines, losing two R-2 tanks. The Division continued the attack to conquer the capital of Moldova, Chişinău, which was captured on 16 July at the cost of one R-2 tank destroyed and five damaged. Having captured Chişinău, the Division's units continued the pursuit of the 95[a] Soviet Rifle Division across the Dnestr to Tighina, captured on 19 July, losing three more R-2 tanks.

▲ General Pantazi inspects the 5th Mechanised Squadron of the 8th[a] Cavalry Division in the Crimea, 8 August 1942, note the crest on the turret with St. George slaying the dragon *(http://www.worldwar2.ro/foto/?id=49&area=31)*

▲ Platoon of R-1 light tanks, belonging to the reconnaissance squadron of a Cavalry Division, advancing towards Odessa in the summer of 1941. Note that the first R-1 is towing the second R-1 with steel cables *(http://tankfront.ru/romania/ photo.html#!prettyPhoto)*

After crossing the Dnestr between 5 and 6 August 1941, the *Divizia 1 Blindată* was assigned to the 4ᵃ Army with the objective of conquering Odessa. The city was protected by two defensive lines and garrisoned by about 100,000 soldiers, with hundreds of cannons and tanks. The Division, starting from the Cârleni-Carantin bridgehead, began the advance towards Odessa together with the 7ᵃ Cavalry Brigade, but the lack of cooperation with the infantry compromised the attack and caused heavy losses. During the fighting that followed the attack from Bujalik towards Odessa between 11 and 14 August, *Regimentul 1 Care de Luptă* lost a total of 47 tanks, including destroyed and damaged tanks.

Regimentul 2 Care de Luptă, after losing half of its R-35 tanks due to mechanical failures during the transfer to the front line, was also involved in the fighting for the conquest of Odessa in support of the I Army Corps units.

As a result of the heavy losses suffered, from 14 August the *Divizia 1 Blindată* was no longer used as an armoured mass, but its tanks were deployed in support of the infantry destined for the attacks on the defences protecting Odessa. The R-2 tanks then took part in the elimination of Soviet firing centres between 14 and 15 August and in the first attack on the city between 16 and 20 August.

▲ A Romanian R-1 light tank captured by the Soviet army near Odessa in September 1941 *(http://wio.ru/tank/romania.htm)*

▼ R-1 light tank platoon, belonging to the mechanised reconnaissance squadron, of a cavalry brigade during the advance into Ukraine in 1941 *(https://thereaderwiki.com/en/R-1_tank)*

▲ An abandoned R-1 light tank near Stalingrad *(https://thereaderwiki.com/en/R-1_tank)*

Here too, the lack of cooperation between infantry and tanks resulted in the loss of numerous tanks: 11 destroyed and 24 damaged. By 20 August, only 20 R-2 tanks remained operational from the 105 tanks present at the start of operations on 2 July. On 21 August, 46 damaged R-2 tanks were transported to Chişinău for repair[17].

The losses suffered in means and men forced the *Divizia 1 Blindată* to proceed to a reorganisation, which led to the establishment of a motorised detachment, with the personnel and means to fight, and the withdrawal from the front to reconstitute the rest of the Division.

The detachment formed, named *'Eftimiu'* after its commander, comprised:

- R-2 Tank Battalion (20 tanks)
- Motorised Hunter Battalion
- Schneider 105 mm cannon group
- Skoda 100 mm howitzer group
- Pioneer Company
- Anti-Aircraft Company 20 mm cannons
- 47 mm anti-tank gun company
- 37 mm anti-aircraft gun battery

---

17 There was a dramatic shortage of field workshops capable of carrying out even the simplest repairs; in almost all cases, damaged or broken-down tanks had to be transported to the rear or to Romania in order to be repaired, resulting in the Regiment's loss of capacity for long periods.

Between 26 and 31 August, the *'Eftimiu'* detachment, subordinate to XI Army Corps, took part in the siege of Odessa, suffering considerable losses, including 11 tanks.

Following the withdrawal of *Regimentul 1 Care de Luptă* from the front, on 1 September 1941, the "*Eftimiu*" detachment was also assigned the surviving R-35 tanks of *Regimentul 2 Care de Luptă* and a battalion of motorised hunters belonging to *Regimentul 3*. It then took part in two more vain attacks to conquer Odessa, so that by 14 September only 10 R-35 tanks remained operational.

On 27 September 1941, the *'Eftimiu'* detachment was reorganised, trained by German instructors and named the 1st Assault Detachment, with the specific task of conducting the final assault to conquer the city. The Assault Detachment consisted of the following units:

- Tank Battalion (12 R-2 and 10 R-35)
- Motorised Hunter Battalion
- Skoda 100 mm howitzer group
- Schneider 105 mm cannon group
- 20 mm anti-aircraft company
- Special Battalion (equipped with flamethrowers, anti-tank guns and mortars)

The 1st Assault Detachment, together with the 7[a] Mixed Cavalry Brigade, went on the attack of the Soviet defensive positions on 16 October 1941, entering Odessa among the first units, which had in the meantime been abandoned by the Soviet garrison by sea during the night. On 24 October, the 1st Assault Detachment was disbanded.

From the entry into the war at the end of June to October 1941, *Divizia 1 Blindată* suffered the following losses: 34 officers, 102 non-commissioned officers, 1,152 soldiers dead, wounded and missing, 206 vehicles and 86 tanks[18]. *Regimentul 1 Care de Luptă* had 26 tanks destroyed, 60 seriously damaged and many more slightly damaged. In contrast, *Regimentul 2 Care de Luptă* lost 15 R-35s and 25 were badly damaged.

With the conquest of the city of Odessa, the first operational cycle of the Romanian armoured forces came to an end; both *Divizia 1 Blindată* and *Regimentul 2 Care de Luptă* were withdrawn from the front and returned to Romania to be reorganised. Recognising the obsolescence of the R-35 tanks, *Regimentul 2 Care de Luptă* was transformed into a training unit in charge of training new tank drivers to replace the losses of *Regimentul 1 Care de Luptă*.

The fighting in which *Divizia 1 Blindată* and *Regimentul 2 Care de Luptă were* involved revealed significant shortcomings in the tactical employment of Romanian armoured vehicles, due to the lack of effective reconnaissance, the erroneous doctrine that still contemplated infantry support even with small groups of tanks and not the use of the armoured mass to break through the adversary's defensive lines, the difficulties of logistics and the lack of field workshops. On the other hand, the fighting valour of the crews and their fighting skills had emerged.

As for the reintegration of the R-2 wagons lost by *Regimentul 1 Care de Luptă*, first the numerous damaged and/or partially destroyed wagons, recovered on the battlefields after the victory, were sent to the workshops: 40 wagons were sent for overhaul to Pilsen and 50 to Ploiești for repairs, between the end of 1941 and January 1942, then new wagons were requested from the German ally, who delivered 26 Pz.Kpfw. 35 (t).

While the R-2 tanks were being restored and overhauled, 62 tanks of different models, 72 light tanks, 38 tracked tractors and 18 Soviet armoured cars were recovered from Bessarabia, Bukovina and Odessa by July 1942. These were used to rebuild 17 tanks, light tanks and armoured cars delivered for training activities in schools and to security units. Recovered parts, armaments and armour were transferred from Transnitria to Romania by dismantling 11 tanks, 29 light tanks and 18 armoured cars. This activity of recovering enemy war material from the battlefields was due to the shortage of

18 According to other sources, losses amounted to 1,261 men, 111 tanks and 220 other vehicles.

▲ Soviet soldiers inspect a Romanian R-1 light tank captured during the battle for the conquest of Odessa in September 1941 *(https://thereaderwiki.com/en/R-1_tank)*

▼ Şenileta Malaxa Tipul UE engaged in the occupation of Bessarabia in July 1941 *(http://tankfront.ru/romania/photo.html#!prettyPhoto)*

raw materials and processed products that had always been lacking in Romania, as well as being a sign of the difficulties in the Romanian manufacturing industry.

Having completed the reorganisation and restoration of means and materials, *Divizia 1 Blindată* returned to the front in the summer of 1942 following the start of operations in southern Russia, being assigned to the Romanian 3rd Army. In the autumn it was deployed on the Don River, northwest of Stalingrad, integrated with two German armoured divisions in the XXXXVIII Panzerkorps, the Axis mobile reserve in the sector. In the confrontation with the Soviet tanks, the R-2 tanks were now outmatched and had no chance of victory in the event of a clash, especially the T-34s, against which the 37-gun shells of the R-2s did not even scratch the armour.

Taking note of the situation, the Germans decided to supply the *Romanians* with some medium-sized wagons, so 11 medium-sized PzKpfw III Ausf. N (T-3 for the Romanians) and as many medium wagons PzKpfw IV Ausf. G (T-4)[19], 10 SdKfz 222 (AB) armoured cars for the reconnaissance unit, 9 PaK 38 5 cm guns and 9 PaK 97/38 7.5 cm guns for the anti-tank battalion.

On the eve of the Battle of Stalingrad, *Divizia 1 Blindată, under* the command of Major General Radu Gheorghe, was composed of:

- Headquarters
- Motorised explorer group
- Military Police Company
- Traffic police platoon
- Transmission Company
- *Regimentul 1 Care de Luptă*

▲ Şenileta Malaxa Tipul UE, with the Schneider 47 light AT gun in tow, parade in Bucharest on the occasion of the taking of Odessa in October 1941 *(http://tankfront.ru/romania/photo.html#!prettyPhoto)*

---

19 T-3 and T-4 tanks were handed over on 17 October to *Regimentul 1 Care de Luptă,* while 1 T-3 and 1 T-4 were handed over to *Regimentul 2 Care de Luptă* for the training of recruits.

- *Regimentul 3.Vanatori Motorizate*
- *Regimentul 4.Vanatori Motorizate*
- *Regiment 1.Artilerie Motorizate*
- Motorised Pioneer Battalion
- Anti-tank battalion
- Anti-aircraft company
- Divisional services

The Division's personnel consisted of: 501 officers, 593 non-commissioned officers, 11,592 soldiers; the armament consisted of 9,335 rifles, 278 machine guns, 61 machine guns, 67 mortars and 36 cannons; the vehicles amounted to 1,358; the number of tanks in its possession were 109 R-2, 11 T-3, 11 T-4, 1 T-60 and 1 BT-7 captured[20], 10 AB and 8 Sd.Kfz. 251.

The *Regimentul 1 Care de Luptă* consisted of two battalions, each with four companies, in the 1st battalion companies 1a - 2a and 3a equipped with R-2 tanks, 4a with the T-4 medium tank, in the 2nd battalion companies 5a - 6a and 7a with R-2s and 8a with the T-3. Only companies 4a and 8a , equipped with T-3 and T-4 medium tanks, were now able to fight on an equal footing against the mass of T-34 and KV tanks held by the Soviet armoured brigades.

In early October 1942, the Division reached the German 6tha Army engaged in the siege of Stalingrad in a long move, during which as many as 12 R-2 tanks were blocked by breakdowns.

The *Divizia 1 Blindată,* with 84 R-2 tanks, 19 T-3 and T-4 tanks and 2 captured Soviet vehicles operational and 37 tanks in the rear under repair, was included in the German XXXXVIII Panzerkorps and deployed near Perelazovsky. On 19 November 1942, the Red Army unleashed Operation Uranus, the gigantic offensive designed to trap the German armies engaged in Stalingrad.

---

20 According to other sources it would be 2 T-26s.

▲ The offensive to conquer Bessarabia begins on 2 July 1941, an R-2 tank advances after crossing the Prut river *(http:// tankfront.ru/romania/photo.html#!prettyPhoto)*

Following the breakthrough made by the Soviets in the front of the 3ᵃ Romanian Army on the Don, on the orders of the XXXXVIII Panzerkorps the *Divizia 1 Blindată* began the movement from Perelazovsky northwards to counter-attack and try to plug the breach. At noon, the XXXXVIII Panzerkorps command was ordered to divert north-west to reach the sector between Blinovsky and Žirkovsky, where it was to attack in the direction of Serafimovič's bridgehead. While the 22ⁿᵈ Panzer-Division carried out the manoeuvre, connections were lost with the *Divizia 1 Blindată,* which then continued north-west, losing all contact with the German units of the XXXXVIII Panzerkorps.

While the German units made contact with the Soviet armoured columns and began a series of battles of uncertain outcome between the afternoons of 19 and 20 November between Blinovsky and Pešcanij, *Divizia 1 Blindată* had finally diverted west to try to rejoin the 22ⁿᵈ Panzer-Division, but at Žirkovsky it was intercepted by two brigades belonging to the Soviet 26ᵗʰ Tank Corps and on 20 November was pushed back eastwards and encircled. The fighting was fierce, losses on both sides were very heavy. The Division claimed the destruction of 62 enemy tanks, losing 25 during the first day of fighting alone. After three days, only 19 R-2 tanks and 11 T-3 and T-4 tanks remained available, but several tanks were damaged and many had to be towed because their fuel had run out. Despite the precarious operational situation, *Divizia 1 Blindată* was assigned the task of attempting to break the encirclement of the 22nd Panzer-Division, an attempt that failed with the further loss of two tanks and 59 vehicles. At the end of November, the remnants of the Division finally managed to break through the encirclement and rejoin the 22. Panzer-Division, and then crossed the Čir River to defend the new line of defence. On 2 December 1942, at the Čir River, *Divizia 1 Blindată* still had two tanks and 944 men on its ranks.

Having received four tanks and 700 men, as well as some light tanks and a few German half-tracks, on 4 December 1942 the remnants of the Division went to form the *Detasamentul Colonel* Nistor (Colonel Nistor's Special Detachment), which continued to fight on the Čir River, preventing the Soviets from crossing the river, but losing all its tanks during the fighting against the 22[a] motorised guard brigade.

In January 1943, all surviving units of *Divizia 1 Blindată* were ordered to return to Romania, where the last contingents arrived in March. Of all the tanks in service at the beginning of November 1942, only 40 were salvageable, almost exclusively R-2s sent to repair workshops in the rear or in Romania. In the cauldron of the Russian steppe also ended the careers of almost all R-1 light tanks, in service with the armoured scout platoons of the cavalry brigades, which were lost in the fighting or due to breakdown[21].

The losses in men and vehicles sustained during the fighting by *Divizia 1 Blindată* in the Don sector were particularly high: 130 officers, 87 non-commissioned officers, 3,067 soldiers, almost 3,000 frozen, 474 rifles, 149 machine guns, 22 machine guns, 55 mortars, 22 cannons, 678 vehicles and 86 tanks. In terms of tank losses, about a third were destroyed by the Soviets, while the rest were abandoned because they were broken down and could not be recovered. In the entire operational cycle on the Don, only one R-2 arrived at the Division as reinforcement in December.

---

21 There is evidence of the use by Romanian cavalry scout units of American M3 Stuart light tanks captured from the Soviets.

▲ *Batalionul care da lupta T-38* Company of *Regimentul 2 Care de Luptă* marching towards the Kuban bridgehead on 13 August 1943 *(http://tankfront.ru/romania/photo.html#!prettyPhoto)*

▲ R-2 tanks camouflaged with branches and branches, belonging to the *Regimentul 1 Care de Luptă* of the *Divizia 1 Blindata*, advancing in Bessarabia in July 1941 *(http://tankfront.ru/romania/photo.html#!prettyPhoto)*

▼ An R-2 tank belonging to *Regimentul 1 Care de Luptă* in flames after being hit by Soviet anti-tanks in Odessa in September 1941 *(http://tankfront.ru/romania/photo.html#!prettyPhoto)*

▲ R-2 tanks belonging to *Divizia 1 Blindată* enter Chişinău, the capital of Moldova, on 16 July 1941 *(https://historice.ro/ armata-romana-si-frontul-de-est-vazute-din-perspectiva-rusa/#jp-carousel-5091)*

▲ A platoon of R-2 tanks from *Regimentul 1 Care de Luptă* drive along a street in Odessa after the capture of the city in September 1941 *(http://tankfront.ru/romania/photo.html#!prettyPhoto)*

▼ R-2 tanks parade in Bucharest during the parade for the conquest of the city of Odessa in October 1941, one can distinctly see the 'cross of Mihai I' in the three colours white-yellow-red painted on the bonnet and, strangely enough given the era, still the coat of arms of King Carol II in the turret *(http://tankfront.ru/romania/photo.html#!prettyPhoto)*

▲ An R-2 tank belonging to the *Divizia 1 Blindată* camouflaged in a forest on the Don front in 1942 *(www.eurasia1945. com/protagonistas/ejercitos/ejercito-real-rumano/)*

▼ R-2 tanks belonging to *Divizia 1 Blindată* advance into Bukovina in July 1941 *(http://wio.ru/tank/romania.htm)*

▲ Damaged R-2 tank No. 234 of *Regimentul 1 Care de Luptă at* Odessa station waiting to be transferred to Ploieşti for repairs, in front an abandoned Soviet BT tank can be seen *(http://tankfront.ru/romania/photo.html#!prettyPhoto)*

▼ An R-2 tank from *Regimentul 1 Care de Luptă* destroyed on the Southern Front *(http://tankfront.ru/romania/photo. html#!prettyPhoto)*

▲ R-2 tank belonging to *Divizia 1 Blindată* during the Battle of Stalingrad in December 1942 *(www.worldwar2.ro/me-dia/?article=366)*

▼ The tank leader of R-2 tank No. 215 belonging to *Regimentul 1 Care de Luptă,* with a damaged rear wheel and left wing, awaits orders to continue the advance in 1941 *(https://bmashine.tumblr.com/image/183624965619)*

▲ R-2 tank No. 234 passes alongside the R-2 tank destroyed by flames in the city of Odessa in September 1941 *(http:// tankfront.ru/romania/photo.html#!prettyPhoto)*

▼ R-2 tank No. 412 belonging to *Regimentul 1 Care de Luptă* on its way to the front in September 1942 (http://tankfront. ru/romania/photo.html#!prettyPhoto)

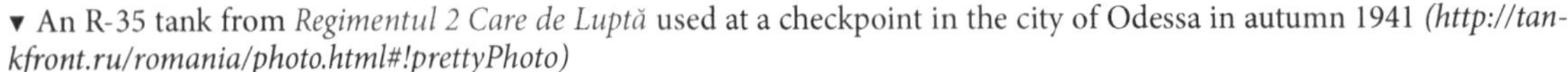

▲ An R-35 tank of *Regimentul 2 Care de Luptă* with its crew, photographed in the city of Odessa in autumn 1941 *(http:// tankfront.ru/romania/photo.html#!prettyPhoto)*

▼ An R-35 tank from *Regimentul 2 Care de Luptă* used at a checkpoint in the city of Odessa in autumn 1941 *(http://tankfront.ru/romania/photo.html#!prettyPhoto)*

▲ R-35 tanks belonging to *Regimentul 2 Care de Luptă* parade in Bucharest on the occasion of the taking of Odessa in October 1941, note the blue band painted around the turret *(https://tanks-encyclopedia.com/ww2/romania/vanatorul-de-care-r35/)*

▲ Romanian soldiers pose with the crew of an R-35 tank belonging to *Regimentul 2 Care de Luptă* in Odessa in autumn 1941 *(http://tankfront.ru/romania/photo.html#!prettyPhoto)*

▼ An R-35 tank belonging to *Regimentul 2 Care de Luptă* drives along a road in Ukraine in 1941 *(http://tankfront.ru/romania/photo.html#!prettyPhoto)*

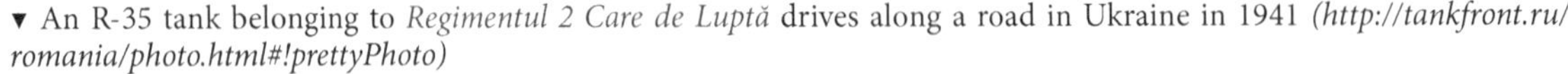

▲ Two R-35 tanks tow a BT-2 captured in Bessarabia in July 1941 *(www.worldwar2.ro/media/?article=366)*

▼ An R-35 tank belonging to *Regimentul 2 Care de Luptă* marching towards Odessa in 1941 *(http://tankfront.ru/romania/photo.html#!prettyPhoto)*

▲ T-3 tank just delivered to *Regimentul 1 Care de Luptă* in 1942 *(http://tankfront.ru/romania/photo.html#!prettyPhoto)*

▼ T-3 tank belonging to the 8ᵃ company of the *Batalionul 2 Care de Lupta - Regimentul 1 Care de Luptă - **Divizia 1 Blindată*** on the Stalingrad front in autumn 1942 *(http://tankfront.ru/romania/photo.html#!prettyPhoto)*

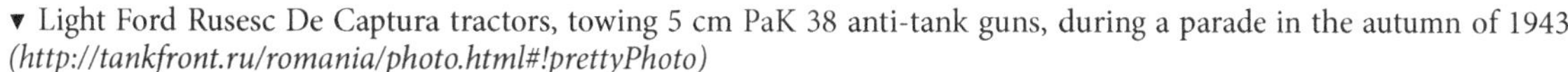

▲ T-3 tank belonging to the 8ᵃ company of *Batalionul 2 Care de Lupta* on the Stalingrad front in autumn 1942 *(from: Armata română și evoluția armei tancuri. Documente (1919-1945)- op. cit. in bibliography)*

▼ Light Ford Rusesc De Captura tractors, towing 5 cm PaK 38 anti-tank guns, during a parade in the autumn of 1943 *(http://tankfront.ru/romania/photo.html#!prettyPhoto)*

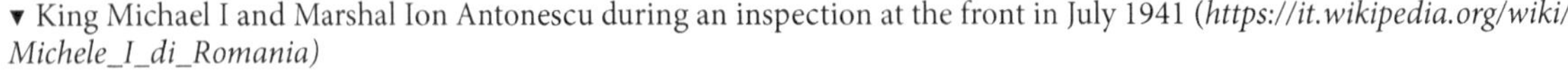

▲ Soviet T-26 tank captured and immediately re-used by the Romanians, note the Michael I Cross painted on the front and sides of the tank as well as the tricolour cockade on the turret hatch (*https://resboiu.wordpress.com/tag/r-2/*)

▼ King Michael I and Marshal Ion Antonescu during an inspection at the front in July 1941 (*https://it.wikipedia.org/wiki/Michele_I_di_Romania*)

▲ T-34/76 tank destroyed by the Romanians and used as an observatory around Stalingrad in the winter of 1942 *(www. worldwar2.ro/media/?article=366)*

▼ Romanian troops pose on an American M3 Lee medium tank surrendered to the Soviets and captured intact in Crimea in 1943 *(www.facebook.com/Count-High-School-Girls-und-Panzer-1548083418836988)*

▲ T-4 tank just delivered to *Regimentul 1 Care de Luptă* in 1942 *(from: Armata română şi evoluţia armei tancuri. Documente (1919-1945)- op. cit. in bibliography)*

▼ An armoured column enters Chişinău, the capital of Bessarabia, in July 1941, motorcyclists on Zündapp KS 600 motorcars precede the R-2 tank column *(http://tankfront.ru/romania/photo.html#!prettyPhoto)*

From Reconstruction to Dissolution - 1943 - 1944

Back home, the reconstruction and reorganisation of *Divizia 1 Blindată began,* firstly recovering all the damaged tanks and sending them to the workshops for appropriate repairs. The materiel situation was extremely critical, as the R-2 tanks, not to mention the R-35s, were now obsolete and unsuitable for countering the Soviet armoured forces equipped with medium and heavy tanks in increasing numbers. In addition to the shortage of adequate tanks, it was necessary to provide for the training of new recruits, the adaptation of operational doctrines that had proved deficient in the first part of the conflict, the replacement of logistical means lost at Stalingrad and the procurement of materials and spare parts.

The main shortage was certainly the lack of modern tanks, which only the Germans could supply, although they did not have them in large quantities. The request for new tanks was accepted by the Germans, although initially with second-hand and outdated vehicles. The other possibility of restoring the supply of tanks, in order to allow the units to return to combat, was to build them themselves, which was difficult due to the lack of industrialisation and the shortage of raw materials. Despite the difficulties, however, during 1943 and 1944, Romanian workshops and industries managed to build a few dozen interesting tanks and fighters, which were used in combat until the end of the conflict.

In early 1943, the MIAPR (Romanian Ministry of Army Equipment and War Production) issued an order for 150 T-3 and T-4 tanks[22] as well as 56 Sturmgeschütz III assault guns.

On 15 April 1943, there were 149 tanks in the *Forţele Terestre Române,* of which 15 R-2, 54 R-35, 1 T-3, 1 T-4. The General Staff was considering the proposal to reconstitute the tank battalions with one company equipped with 88-mm cannon tanks and two companies with T-4 tanks, a proposal that was absolutely acceptable given the quality of the Soviet tanks to be faced, but unfeasible due to the economic costs and the difficulty of obtaining the necessary means from the German ally.

In the second fortnight of April 1943, the following vehicles were delivered by the Germans: 164 cars, 172 trucks, 56 tractors, 21 ambulances and 50 PzKpfw 38(t) tanks (T-38 for the Romanians), the latter coming directly from Škoda after being overhauled. Between May and August, 12 R-2s were repaired at the divisional workshop, bringing the number of operational tanks to 27 out of the 61 in charge.

With the 50 PzKpfw 38(t), received in March 1943[23], it was the intention of the Romanian army to establish three light tank companies to be included in three cavalry divisions as scouting divisions, but the Wehrmacht imposed, as a condition of sale, the delivery to divisions directly engaged at the front in the Crimea. Thus, the *Batalionul care da lupta T-38* of *Regimentul 2 Care de Luptă was* formed, consisting of three companies: 51, 52 and 53 each with 15 T-38 tanks, as well as five T-38s held in reserve at battalion headquarters. These consisted of tanks Ausf. A, Ausf. B and Ausf. C wagons that were worn out, even though they had been overhauled by the company, and were now obsolete and unsuitable for comparison with Soviet vehicles; furthermore, on their arrival at the battalion headquarters, it was found that only 17 were operational, while the other 33 needed heavy maintenance! The *Batalionul care da lupta T-38,* operational since June 1943 and assigned to the Cavalry Corps, was sent to the Kuban bridgehead to support the trapped Romanian forces. During the first fighting, seven T-38s were lost to anti-tank guns and Soviet infantry attacks.

Following the retreat of the Axis units, the *Batalionul care da lupta T-38* reached the Crimea, where it took part in heavy fighting until early 1944, when the survivors of Companies 51 and 52 were evacuated by ship to Romania, with only 10 operational T-38s[24]. With the five T-38s from the battalion command in the winter of 1943/44, Company 54 was formed.

---

22 Although it was initially planned to order T-3 tanks as well, in reality only T-4 tanks were delivered.
23 According to another source the Panzer 38(t) were delivered between 15 May and 24 June 1943.
24 Other sources indicate that in April 1944 there were still 10 T-38s from Company 53 supporting the 10th Infantry Division in the Crimea.

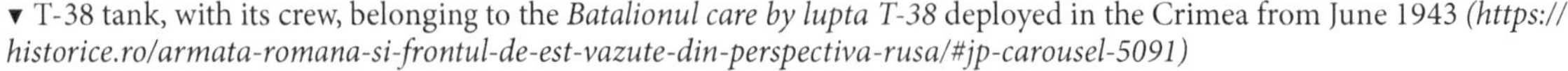

▲ T-38 tanks belonging to the *Batalionul care by lupta T-38* marching towards the Kuban bridgehead in the summer of 1943 *(http://tankfront.ru/romania/photo.html#!prettyPhoto)*

▼ T-38 tank, with its crew, belonging to the *Batalionul care by lupta T-38* deployed in the Crimea from June 1943 *(https://historice.ro/armata-romana-si-frontul-de-est-vazute-din-perspectiva-rusa/#jp-carousel-5091)*

The delivery of these materials, whether tanks or armoured vehicles or trucks, had by no means solved the shortage of equipment that prevented the reestablishment of the *Divizia 1 Blindată* fighting units. Therefore, on 23 September 1943[25] a new armament programme was approved, including the supply of tanks, assault cannons, armoured and motorised vehicles, called "Olivenbaum", with which to restore the operation of *Divizia 1 Blindată.* as well as providing the vehicles for the Motorised Troops Command, the 1st Armoured Training Division and the transformation of the 8a motorised cavalry division into a new armoured division called *Divizia 2 blindată* (2a Armoured Division). All these new units were part of the programme of the Reorganisation Law of the Romanian Armed Forces. The "Olivenbaum" programme was followed by "Olivenbaum II" and "Olivenbaum III", all of which were completed between the end of 1943 and the summer of 1944.

Deliveries were very slow, in 1943 only 31 T-4s and 4 Sturmgeschütz III Ausf. G (T.As. T3 for the Romanians) while by August 1944 a further 83 T-4s[26] and 104 T.As. T3. The T-4s were mainly of the type Ausf. H and Ausf. J, but at least 32 were second-hand and worn, as they came from the 23.Panzer-division.

In addition to the tanks foreseen in the agreed programmes, Germany also promised to deliver 3 Panzerbefehlswagen IV command wagons, 40 Sd.Kfz.222 armoured cars, 8 Italian AB 41 armoured cars captured after 8 September, 45 Sd.Kfz.250 half-tracks (called light SPWs) and 27 Sd.Kfz.251/1 Ausf. D (medium SPW).

While the purchase of German tanks and assault cannons proceeded albeit slowly, the need to reinforce armoured units and replace antiquated vehicles was increasingly a priority for the leadership of the *Forțele Terestre Române*. Using the cannons and tanks captured from the Soviets, the few national industries capable of designing and producing armoured vehicles and the technical skills of Colonel Ghiulai, a number of interesting tank fighters were designed and subsequently built and used until the end of the conflict.

The first vehicle designed in 1942 was the **TACAM R-1** 'Tun Anticar pe Afet Mobil' (anti-tank gun on a mobile device), using the R-1 light tank as a base on which to install a Soviet 45 mm M1937 cannon. The official proposal for the conversion of 14 R-1s into TACAM R-1s to the *Forțele Terestre Române* was sent in 1943, but was rejected as the 45 mm cannon was now obsolete and unsuitable for countering Soviet tanks.

In 1943, the **TACAM T-38 was designed**, which involved the conversion of the PzKpfw 38(t) into a tank destroyer, installing the 76.2 mm Soviet F-22 cannon, captured in numerous examples from the Romanians, and using armour recovered from captured Soviet vehicles for the armour. This project, very similar to the German Marder III, also remained on paper as, by the time it was accepted in 1944, Romania had changed allies and all captured Soviet equipment had been confiscated and recovered by the new allies.

While the first two projects remained on paper, the new programme turned out to be feasible and even discreet from an operational point of view: the **TACAM T-60** 'Tun Anticar pe Afet Mobil/ Tun autopropulsat cu Afet Mobile' (anti-tank gun on a mobile device/self-propelled gun on a mobile device) . Having dozens and dozens of 76.2 mm F-22 cannons and more than 100 T-60 light tanks, captured from the Soviets in the first years of the war, and in view of the need to equip the armoured units with means up to the situation, in 1942, engineer Lieutenant-Colonel Constantin Giulai proposed the transformation of the captured T-60s into tank destroyers. The Command of the *Forțele Terestre Române* accepted the proposal and construction of the prototype began.

The conversion involved the removal of the turret, the turret platform and the construction of a

---

25 According to some sources, the Law for the Reorganisation of the Armed Forces was promulgated on 28 October 1943.
26 The total number of Panzerkampfwagen IV delivered from Germany to Romania is still a source of uncertainty, the number of 126 T-4s delivered is considered to be the number that comes closest to reality, but for some sources the number fluctuates between 114 and 127, for others between 129 or 131, or 108 or 114 and finally 118 or 120.

▲ Two Batalionul T-38 tanks abandoned in the Crimea in autumn 1943 (*http://tankfront.ru/romania/photo.html#!prettyPhoto*)

superstructure open from above and behind, built from 15 mm thick armoured plates obtained by dismantling captured BT-7 tanks, protected above from the weather by a canvas laid over a tube frame. A 76.2 mm F-22 cannon with 44 rounds of ammunition was positioned in the casemate, with seats for the commander/gunner and servant, while the pilot's post was moved to the left and protected with external armour. A 7.92 mm ZB vz 37 machine gun, carried inside the casemate, formed the defensive armament against enemy infantry. To better support the increased weight, the original suspension was improved by installing stronger torsion bars and new wheels, while minor improvements were made to the engine. The prototype was built at the Leonida factory in Bucharest and finished on 19 January 1943. The prototype was immediately accepted and the conversion of the T-60s already delivered to the Leonid into the new fighter began immediately. In total, 34 TACAM T-60s were built by Leonida, 17 were finished in the first half of 1943 and the other 17 in the second half.

The TACAM T-60s made their first public appearance during the parade held in Bucharest on 10 May 1943, and were then sent to the Centrului de instructie Mecanizat (Mechanized Training Centre) and *Regimentul 1 Care de Luptă in* June, for crew training. At the end of the year, two *Compania de Vânători de tancuri* (Tank Hunters Company) were established: 61[a] in *Regimentul 1 Care de Luptă*, equipped with 16 TACAM T-60s, and 62[a] in *Regimentul 2 Care de Luptă* with 18 vehicles.

The baptism of fire for the TACAM T-60 came in February 1944, when two batteries equipped with 14 fighters, framed in the 'Cantemir' Detachment, were involved in the fighting in defence of northern Transnistria.

As the R-2 tanks were now considered unusable, in the spring of 1943, General Pantazi ordered that the still operational R-2s should be converted into self-propelled guns, equipped with armament capable of fighting Soviet armoured tanks on an equal footing. For the conversion of the R-2 into self-propelled guns, Lieutenant Colonel Ghiulai was again commissioned, drawing on the experience gained from the construction of the TACAM T-60. The first prototype was completed in the summer of 1943 at the Leonidas factory and named the **TACAM R-2** 'Tun Anticar pe Afet Mobil R-2'.

▲ Infantry training in anti-tank fighting using T-38 tanks *(www.worldwar2.ro/media/?article=366)*

▼ Vânători Motorizate, belonging to *Divizia 1 Blindată, on* board medium SPWs during training in spring 1944 *(https://m.facebook.com/groups/1045025415560649/permalink/1233119916751197/)*

▲ General Radu Korne, commander of the *Divizia România Mare,* standing on the right in the half-track observing the division's field manoeuvres in April 1944 (*www.avalanchepress.com/RomaniaMare.php*)

The structure of the TACAM R-2 followed that of the TACAM T-60, with a 76.2 mm F22 cannon installed inside a superstructure, partially open at the top and rear, made from armoured plates cut from captured T-26 and BT tanks and located at the front of the vehicle. The prototype was tested in late 1943 at Suditi, demonstrating its full potential and capability. The Romanian Command then ordered that all R-2 tanks in service be promptly converted to TACAM R-2s. However, this order was immediately blocked by the commander of *Divizia 1 Blindată*, because he demanded the delivery of replacement tanks before handing over the R-2s in service. This setback blocked the conversion of the R-2s into TACAM R-2s until February 1944!

The delivery of the R-2s to the Leonid factory for conversion was finally released, but further delays resulted from the delayed delivery of some components by the Germans, so that series production did not begin until the end of February. In the meantime, the decision had matured to replace the F-22 cannon with the M1942, or ZiS-3 cannon, which had better ballistic properties and 30 projectiles ready for use. A total of 20 TACAM R-2s were produced by the end of July 1944, in addition to the prototype, 7 of which were transferred to the Mihai Bravu training centre.

In July 1944, at *Regimentul 1 Care de Luptă*, the 5[a] TACAM R-2 company was established in Batalion 2.Care de Lupta, which later became 63[a] Anti-Tank Company.

The last project for a national destroyer, developed by a committee in which both military and civilian personnel were present, was the Mareşal, a light destroyer named Mareşal in honour of Marshal Antonescu, who supported the project and closely followed the development and field trials.

The first prototype of the Mareşal, named M-00, built on the basis of the design drawn up by the committee, consisted of a 122 mm Soviet M1910/1930 howitzer, with a 7.92 mm ZB-53 coaxial machine gun, mounted on a chassis based on the T-60, where the original turret and frame had been replaced by a superstructure with highly inclined plates, powered by a Ford V8 engine. The prototype was quickly finished and sent for testing on 30 July 1943, showing serious shortcomings

▲ A T-4 tank belonging to *Regimentul 1 Care de Luptă* on its way to the front in spring 1944 *(https://m.facebook.com/groups/1045025415560649/permalink/1233119916751197/)*

and defects, especially in the armament and engine. The engineers at Rogifer, formerly Malaxa, set to work feverishly and in just three months were able to build three more prototypes: M-01, M-02 and M-03.

Although quite similar to the previous M-00, the new prototypes were larger, with reinforced suspension and fitted with 120 hp Buick engines, while the armament remained unchanged. Tested in Suditi on 23 October 1943, in the presence of Marshal Antonescu, they still demonstrated the same problems with the howitzer, which was too heavy for the T-60 chassis. As the new 75 mm Reşiţa Model 1943 anti-tank gun had been tested at the same time, which had proved very well, it was proposed to replace the 122 mm howitzer with the new Reşiţa gun, while for the engine, it was planned to replace the Ford engine with a 120 hp Hotchkiss.

The new M-04 prototype, equipped with the 75-mm cannon, was sent for trials in February 1944, with positive results, but, in March 1944, it was decided to replace the T-60 tank platform, used until then, with that of the T-38. The M-05 and M-06 prototypes were then built on the basis of the T-38 tank and sent for testing. Collaboration was also established between Romanian and German engineers, mainly from Vomag and Alkett, deciding that the production Mareşal would have the French engine, Czechoslovak BMM suspension, Romanian gun and superstructure, and German optics and radios. The improved M-06 prototype was quickly built and tested in May, and in July it was presented to Marshal Antonescu. The order for serial construction was then signed, along with an agreement with Germany for the supply of materials and a licence to produce the Praga AC engine. The slow supply of materials and Allied aerial bombardment against the factories identified for construction delayed the start of series production of the Mareşal, forcing the Romanian Command to cancel the project. The Soviets in September 1944 confiscated all construction plans and the M-05 prototype, writing the word end of the Mareşal.

In addition to designing and building fighters from conversions of existing or new wagons, in the years between late 1942 and early 1944, some modifications, even significant ones, were made to wagons and vehicles in service in an attempt to improve their operability.

▲ A damaged T-4 tank used for crew training (*https://m.facebook.com/groups/1045025415560649/perma-link/1233119916751197/*)

By the end of 1943, fifty Şenileţă Malaxa Tip UE remained operational, of which 33 were used for training purposes while seventeen were reconditioned by the Malaxa factory, between January and the end of March 1944, to be capable of towing the German 5 cm PaK 38 anti-tank gun.

During the first months of the campaign against the Soviet Union, the Romanian army captured several dozen T-20 Komsomolec light artillery tractors, most of them in poor condition. Thirty-four of them were shipped to Romania, which were first reconditioned by Rogifer in Bucharest and then transferred to Uzina Parvan Marian, where towing hooks were installed to enable them to tow German 5 cm PaK 38 anti-tank guns. Work began in the spring of 1943 and was completed in the autumn of the same year. The completed tractors were named **Ford Rusesc De** Captura (Russian Capture Ford). Almost all the tractors were lost on the Moldavian front in the summer of 1944, the few surviving Ford Rusesc De Capturas were confiscated by the Soviets after 23 August 1944.

Towards the end of 1942, noting the obsolescence of the R-35, the command of *Regimentul 2 Care de Luptă* proposed to rearm the surviving tanks, equipped with the original obsolete Puteaux SA 18 cannon, with a 47 mm Schneider cannon. Instead, the Ministry of Defence chose to install the 45 mm 20K L/46 cannon, which was present in large numbers following the capture of several Soviet T-26 and BT tanks. The project was officially started on 12 December 1942, entrusted to Lieutenant Colonel Ghiulai assisted by Captain Hogea. In January 1943, the new gun mount was designed, but the idea of also fitting a machine gun had to be abandoned because, due to the size of the gun, there was not enough space.

The prototype, assembled at the Concordia factory in Ploieşti, was finished in February 1943 and immediately sent to the field to test its behaviour on the ground. The tests revealed the good ballistic capabilities of the 20K L/46 cannon, but also the poor speed and acceleration due to the inadequacy of the original 80 hp Renault V4 engine. Despite this, the tank was accepted and put into production under the name **Vanatorul de Care R-35**. A total of 30 R-35s were converted to the Vanatorul de Care R-35, all delivered by 1943, a further batch was planned but, due to the destruction of the factory by aerial bombing, was scrapped.

▲ T-4 tank belonging to *Regimentul 1 Care de Luptă* under repair at a field workshop, note the German camouflage scheme, as the tank had belonged to the 23. Panzer-Division in 1944 (*www.worldwar2.ro/media/?article=366*)

▲ A T-4 tank belonging to *Regimentul 1 Care de Luptă* during training in 1943.
(https://m.facebook.com/groups/1045025415560649/permalink/1233119916751197/)

▼ A T.As. assault cannon. T3 advances through the mud in the spring of 1944 *(http://tankfront.ru/romania/photo.html#!prettyPhoto)*

While the rearmament and reorganisation of the *Divizia 1 Blindată*[27], the *Regimentul 2 Care de Luptă* and the transformation of the 8[a] Motorised Cavalry Division into a new Armoured Division proceeded, albeit slowly, the fighting raged closer and closer to Romania's borders, following the continued victorious Soviet offensives.

In order to face the advance of the Soviet units, in February 1944, the *"Grupul mixt blindat Cantemir"* (Cantemir Armoured Mixed Group) was formed with the ready-to-use units belonging to *Divizia 1 Blindată* and immediately sent to the Moldavian front. It consisted of two tank companies with 30 T-4s and 2 T-3s, one assault gun company with 10 T.As. T3, two tank batteries with 14 TACAM T-60s, one company with R-2 tanks and one with R-35 tanks. The *Grupul mixt armouredat Cantemir* remained at the front until April 1944, when it returned to Romania and the surviving vehicles returned to their units. Upon returning to the Division, a tank battalion was formed, with a battery of TACAM T-60s and a battery of T.As. T3 battery, where each battery consisted of three platoons, each consisting of three tank destroyers, or assault guns, plus one for the commander, making a total of 10 vehicles per battery, one armoured car, one passenger car and 14 supply and service trucks.

On 28 March, the *"Detasamentul Blindat Rapid"* (Rapid Armoured Detachment) was formed, again with units from *Divizia 1 Blindată,* consisting of a tank battalion in two companies with 32 T-4s and one company with 12 T.As. T3, the 63[a] anti-tank battery with 7 TACAM T-60, a motorised infantry battalion, an artillery group with 12 Skoda 100 mm guns, an anti-tank company with 6 75 mm Reşiţa Model 1943 guns, an anti-aircraft company and support units. The *Detasamentul Blindat Rapid* sustained heavy fighting against Soviet units in Moldavia, returning to Romania towards the end of April.

On 7 April 1944, with units from the 8[a] Motorised Cavalry Division, the 'Cojocaru' Battle Group was formed, comprising the 12th Motorised Regiment, the 3rd Motorised Artillery Regiment, three independent infantry battalions and three TACAM T-60 tank destroyers of the 62[a] company. The 'Cojocaru' Group remained operational until 30 June 1944, when it was disbanded and the units returned to their home units.

On 28 April 1944, the reconstruction of *Divizia 1 Blindată* was completed, returning to operation under the new name of *Divizia România Mare* (Greater Romania Division), which, at the beginning of August, had the following structure:

* Headquarters
* Exploring Company
* Batalionul de Pionieri Moto
* *Regimentul 1 Care de Luptă*
* *Regimentul 3.Vanatori Motorizate*
* *Regiment 1.Artilerie Motorizate*
* Anti-Aircraft Artillery Company
* Divizionul de Artilerie Antitanc
* Various services

With a staff of 11,870 officers, NCOs and soldiers, it was equipped with 48 T-4s, 22 T.As. T3, 10 TACAM T-60, 30 AB, 20 SPW 251, 780 light/medium/heavy trucks, 140 passenger cars, 24 Schwimmwagen.

While the most high-performance vehicles were sent to the front, 44 R-2 tanks still remained available in Romania in July 1944, which, in view of their obsolescence, were allocated to the training of the new tank units.

---

27 At the end of 1943, 64 R-2 tanks were in the charge of Divizia 1 Blindată, of which 51 were in need of repair, while there were 54 R-35 tanks operating at Regimentul 2 Care de Luptă and the Târgovişte Motorised Training Centre.

▲ A T.As. assault cannon. T3 assault gun during training in the winter of 1943 *(from: Armata română şi evoluţia armei tancuri. Documente (1919-1945)- op. cit. in bibliography)*

In August 1944, the Red Army unleashed the offensive on the Southern Front with the aim of occupying Romania and continuing the advance towards the Balkans. The Romanian armoured forces available to face the Soviet units were the *Divizia România Mare,* with 48 T-4 tanks and 32 T.As. assault/tank guns. T3 and TACAM T-60, and the 8[a] Motorised Cavalry Division, with 30 T-4 tanks and 21 T.As.T3 assault guns.

On 12 August, the *România Mare Division* was sent to the area of Iaşi, to try to counter the offensive that the Soviets had launched in Bessarabia. Due to the occupation by Soviet troops of the villages of Cosinţeni, Zmeu, Crucea and Popeşti, the Division was divided into two groups: one in the Hărpăşeşti area and the other in Sineşti. In the afternoon of 20 August, the *Divizia România Mare* carried out a counterattack against the Soviets' western flank, but failed to break through the enemy's defensive line. In the battle, the Soviets suffered the loss of 60 tanks, while the Romanians lost a total of 35 tanks and trucks. General Radu Korné, commander of the Division, in the night of 20-21 August 1944 ordered the establishment of two operational detachments: in the Sinteşti area under the command of Colonel Constantinescu and in the Hărpăşeşti area under the command of Colonel Nistor. The two detachments remained in contact with the Soviet troops, carrying out rearguard duties during the Division's retreat during the night of 22-23 August 1944. Engaged in fierce fighting, faced with an overwhelming numerical and material superiority of the enemy, the Division retreated within the pre-war border, having lost, by 23 August, 30 T-4 tanks and 20 T.As. T-3 and TACAM T-60.

The 8[a] Motorised Cavalry Division, however, could not contribute to the defence with its armoured vehicles, as these were taken by the Germans from a kampfgruppe of the 20. Panzer-Division.

▲ A T.As. assault cannon. T3 assault gun during training with German instructors *(https://477768.livejournal.com/tag/ Румыния)*

▼ Vânători Motorizate, in a moment of rest, resting under the shelter of a T.As. assault cannon. T3 assault cannon in the winter of 1944 *(https://historice.ro/armata-romana-si-frontul-de-est-vazute-din-perspectiva-rusa/#jp-carousel-5091)*

▲ Vânători Motorizate, in a moment of rest, resting under the shelter of a T.As. assault cannon. T3 assault cannon in the winter of 1944 *(https://historice.ro/armata-romana-si-frontul-de-est-vazute-din-perspectiva-rusa/#jp-carousel-5091)*

▼ On 10 May 1943, during the National Day parade held in Bucharest, TACAM T-60s paraded for the first time *(https:// thearmoredpatrol.com/2018/08/18/romanian-tanks-in-detail-tacam-t-60-t-60a/)*

▲ Another image of TACAM T-60, during the National Day parade held in Bucharest on 10 May 1943 *(https://thearmore-dpatrol.com/2018/08/18/romanian-tanks-in-detail-tacam-t-60-t-60a/)*

▼ A TACAM T-60 during training, note the tube frame on which a tarp could be placed to shelter the crew from the weather *(www.tankarchives.ca/2016/09/tacam-t-60-spg-transylvanian-style.html)*

▲ A TACAM T-60 abandoned by the Romanians after being hit during the defence of Transnitria in March 1944 *(https:// thearmoredpatrol.com/2018/08/18/romanian-tanks-in-detail-tacam-t-60-t-60a/)*

▼ A unique photograph, unfortunately of poor quality, of a TACAM T-60 with the protective tarpaulin laid down to protect the casemate *(http://beutepanzer.ru/Beutepanzer/su/Romania/tacam_t-60_1.htm)*

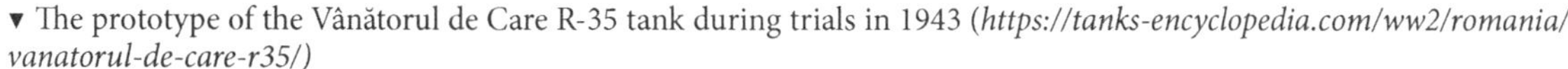

▲ A TACAM T-60, belonging to the *'Grupul mixt blindat Cantemir'*, lurking between houses ready to fire on the Moldavian front in the spring of 1944 (*https://daydaynews.cc/en/military/605814.html*)

▼ The prototype of the Vânătorul de Care R-35 tank during trials in 1943 (*https://tanks-encyclopedia.com/ww2/romania/vanatorul-de-care-r35/*)

▲ Romanian tank driver posing in front of his Vânătorul de Care R-35 tank in the winter of 1943 (*www.facebook.com/Count-High-School-Girls-und-Panzer-1548083418836988*)

▼ Dimensioned drawing of prototype No. 6 of the Mareşal tank destroyer, with the date of receipt by the military organs of 4 April 1944 (*www.deviantart.com/wingsofwrath/art/TACAB-General-Plan-204061718*)

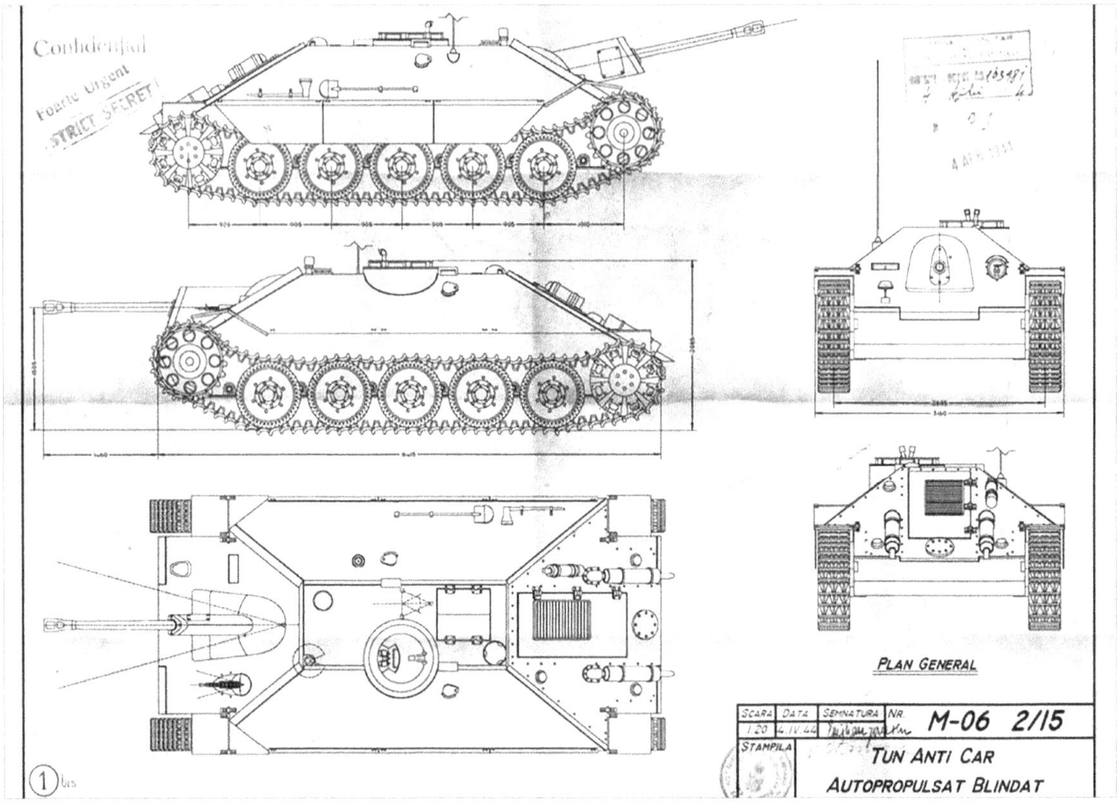

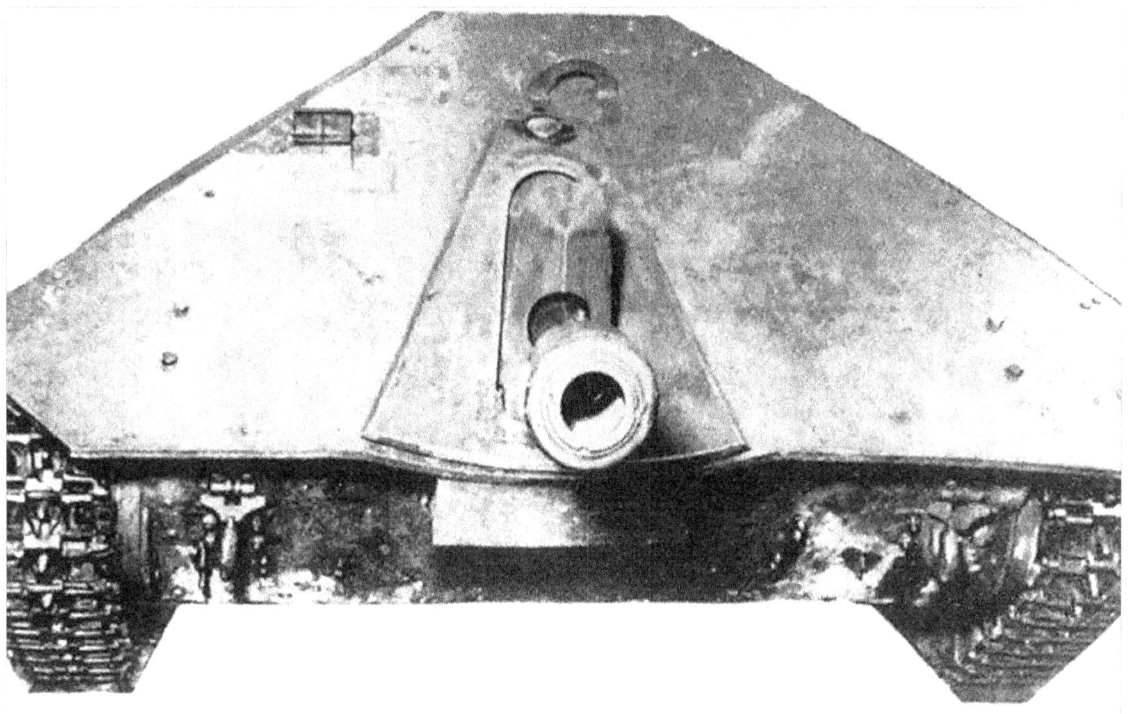

▲ The prototype M-04 Mareşal tank destroyer with 75 mm Reşiţa Model 1943 anti-tank gun in February 1944 *(www. facebook.com/Count-High-School-Girls-und-Panzer-1548083418836988)*

▼ View of the interior of the M-04 prototype of the Mareşal fighter under construction at Rogifer in Bucharest *(www. facebook.com/Count-High-School-Girls-und-Panzer-1548083418836988)*

▲ Another view of the interior of the M-04 prototype Mareşal fighter under construction *(www.facebook.com/Count-High-School-Girls-und-Panzer-1548083418836988)*

From the Armistice of 23 August 1944 to the end of the war

By the beginning of 1944 it was clear what the outcome of the war would be, King Michael I and the Romanian political and military forces, in favour of a truce with the Soviet Union to avoid the devastation of a war on home soil, began to make contact with the Allies, informing them of the intention to dismiss Marshal Antonescu's government by means of a coup d'état, sign an armistice and deploy the army against the former German allies. Generals and officers from the reserve divisions, the commander and garrison of Bucharest, as well as democratic and communist politicians to be installed in the new democratic government were involved in the preparation of the coup.

In the early afternoon of 23 August, Marshal Antonescu was arrested on the orders of King Michael I, who immediately afterwards sent a telegram to the military command in Cairo informing the Allies of the coup and, at 10 p.m., announced on the radio the truce with the Soviets and the declaration of war against Germany. While in Bucharest the population took to the streets to celebrate the end of the war against the Soviets, the city's garrison prepared to neutralise the Germans.

By the evening of 23 August 1944, the majority of the Romanian armoured forces were on the front in Moldova, where the situation in the *Divizia România Mare* was critical, with *Regimentul 1 Care de Luptă* deployed in Gheboieni-Dâmboviţa. while *Regimentul 2 Care de Luptă* was in the capital and 16 tanks were at the Motomechanized Training Centre in Târgovişte. Numerous vehicles were then at the factories and workshops to carry out repairs, overhauls or conversions into the newly designed vehicles, not to mention the presence of old FT17s in the barracks.

Following the truce with the Soviet Union[28], the *Divizia România Mare* was ordered to retreat southwards, but was surrounded and captured almost entirely by the Soviets on 24 August[29]. After negotiations with the Soviet side held on 27 August in the Buda-Şipote locality, the Division's command managed to obtain the establishment of a detachment, formed with the units of the *Divizia România Mare,* that would fight against the Germans alongside the Soviet units.

At the end of August, the *Detasamentul Blindat 'Gheorghe Matei'*, named after the commanding lieutenant colonel, was formed, with the primary objective of liberating the whole of Transylvania, and consisted of the following units:

- Batalion *Regimentul 3.Vanatori Motorizate*
- Batalion Care de Lupta - tank company (9 T-4); assault gun company (7 T.As. T3)
- 101ᵃ anti-tank company
- a pioneer company
- an anti-aircraft company
- various services

a total of 1,058 soldiers, 16 tanks and assault guns, 33 cannons and mortars, 133 vehicles, including trucks and cars.

The Detasamentul Blindat "Gheorghe Matei" fought under Soviet command, as part of the 24th Guards Corps, contributing to the liberation of Transylvania until 28 September, when it returned under the command of the Romanian Army. During his operational activity, between 30 August and 28 September 1944, he achieved the following military objectives:

- conquest of the Ghimeş-Palanca Pass
- pursuit of the enemy beyond Sovata
- conquest of Reghin.

---

28 The armistice between the Soviet Union and Romania was officially signed on 12 September.
29 According to some memoirs, the entire TACAM T-60 unit in service was captured by the Soviet army between 20 and 25 August 1944 and the crews were taken prisoner.

As of 28 September, the Detasamentul Blindat 'Gheorghe Matei' not only inflicted heavy losses on the enemy, but also boasted the capture of 1,800 prisoners and 8 tanks, compared to only 5 tanks lost or damaged.

For the defence of the capital and the oil installations in Ploieşti, two armoured detachments were created with personnel and vehicles from the *Divizia România Mare,* the *Regimentul 2 Care de Luptă* and the Motomechanized Training Centre in Târgovişte. On 24 August 1944, the *Detaşamentul Blindat* General Niculescu (General Niculescu Armoured Detachment) was formed[30], part of the General Rozin Motorised Corps, with the following units:

- Exploratory group
- Batalion Care de Lupta - tank company (10 T-4); assault gun company (10 T.As. T3)
- Batalion Vânătorul de tancuri (12 TACAM R-2)
- Batalion *Regimentul 4.Vanatori Motorizate*
- Anti-tank company

The Detaşamentul Blindat General Niculescu participated in the battle for the liberation of Bucharest, then in the fighting to drive the Germans out of Baneasa and Otopeni and then, incorporated into the Motorised Corps, was sent to Transylvania where it fought in Oarba de Mures. At the end of its deployment in Transylvania on 28 September 1944, it was disbanded.

Also on 24 August 1944, another small armoured unit was formed: the *Detaşamentul Blindat 'Popescu'* (Armoured Detachment Popescu) named after its commander Major Victor Popescu, with the following personnel:

---

30 *Detaşamentul Blindat General Niculescu* was also referred to as Armoured Detachment 'Jupiter'.

▲ At *Regimentul 2 Care de Luptă* an interesting modification was made, installing the turret of a Soviet T-26 tank on an R-35 tank. This is the only existing photograph of the vehicle, transported on a railway flatbed probably seized by the Soviets in October 1944 (*www.facebook.com/Count-High-School-Girls-und-Panzer-1548083418836988*)

- R-2 Armoured Company
- T-38 Platoon
- R-35 Platoon/Vanatorul de Care R-35
- Motorized Vanators
- Anti-tank and anti-aircraft training groups

The Detaşamentul Blindat Popescu took an active part in the fighting for the liberation of the Ploieşti oil zone until 31 August 1944, when it was disbanded.

During the fighting sustained by the Romanian troops against the Germans after 23 August 1944, the decrepit FT17s were also used for the protection of institutional premises or industrial plants in Bucharest, Ploiesti, Sibiu and Resita. Despite their obsolescence, they still managed to be decisive in many cases in eliminating pockets of German resistance in the locations where they were operational[31].

In application of the agreements provided for in the armistice protocols with the Soviet Union, at the end of September, the Command of the *România Mare Division* received order No. 67,000, from the General Staff, ordering the reduction of personnel to the bare minimum. The reduction was implemented by dismissing most of the serving personnel, the first stage of its definitive disbandment. The armistice clauses obliged the *Forţele Terestre Române* to disband, within 35 days, several military structures and units: an army command, four army corps commands and 14 divisions; one of these was the *Divizia România Mare,* born as *Divizia 1 Blindată* only in 1941[32]. The official disbandment order came with Order No. 70.220 on 1 November 1944, stipulated that the personnel belonging to *Regimentul 3.Vanatori Motorizate* and *Regimentul 4.Vanatori Motorizate* would merge into the 2[a] Mountain Division, while *Regimentul 1 Care de Luptă* would be merged with *Regimentul 2 Care de Luptă,* which thus remained the only Romanian armoured force in service. As stipulated in the Vinogradov-Rădescu Protocol, the reorganisation of the units concerned was completed by 1 December 1944.

With elements of the *Detasamentul Blindat 'Gheorghe Matei'* and the *Detaşamentul Blindat General Niculescu* on 1 October 1944[33] the *Grupul Blindat al Armatei 4 romane* (Armoured Group of the Romanian 4[a] Army) was formed, consisting of the following units:

Batalion Care de Lupta - tank company (10 T-4); assault gun company (8 T.As. T3)

Batalion Vânătorul de tancuri (16 TACAM R-2)

The Grupul Blindat al Armatei 4 romane took part in the fighting in the final phase of the offensive for the liberation of Transylvania[34], fighting against Germans and Hungarians until it reached the Tisza River in Hungary. During the violent clashes with the enemy, 10 TACAM R-2s were destroyed. The Grupul Blindat al Armatei 4 Romane was disbanded in November 1944.

With the disbanding of the Grupul Blindat al Armatei 4 Romane, the operational activity of the Romanian armoured units came to an end. The only unit that survived the 'reorganisation' imposed by the Soviets was *Regimentul 2 Care de Luptă,* which during the conflict, apart from its initial participation in the fighting for the conquest of Odessa, had acted as a training centre and replacement training for the *Divizia 1 Blindată. The Regimentul 2 Care de Luptă was* then

---

31 In February 1945 all FT17s were seized by the Soviet army and transferred to the Soviet Union, only one FT17 remained in Romania and is now in the Military Museum in Bucharest.

32 In addition to the dissolution of military structures and departments, the armistice clauses also included an article in which it was stipulated that all Soviet vehicles and armaments, captured by the Romanians during the war, would be requisitioned and returned to the Soviet Union, including those resulting from conversions such as the TACAM T-60, an example of which was tested at Kubinka.

33 Other sources give the date of 4 October 1944 as the date of establishment of the *Grupul Blindat al Armatei 4 romane.*

34 During the liberation of Transylvania, two Hetzers and a functioning Zrinny II were captured and used by Romanian tank drivers until their seizure by the Soviets in November 1944.

restructured so that it could be deployed alongside Red Army units in the final phase of the conflict, especially in the fighting for the liberation of Czechoslovakia and Austria.

When *Regimentul 2 Care de Luptă* was sent to the front in Czechoslovakia in February 1945, it had the following organisation:

- Headquarters Company - radio communications platoon, cable communications platoon, pioneer platoon
- Explorer Group - 8 AB[35] and 5 SPW[36]
- Batalionul 1 Tancuri - one tank company (8 T-4), 2 assault gun companies (13 T.As. T3[37])
- Batalionul 2 Tancuri Uşoare (2nd Light Tank Battalion) - 2 R-35 tank companies (28 R-35 and Vanatorul de Care R-35), 1 T-38 tank company (9 T-38) and 1 TACAM battery (5 TACAM R-2)
- Tank explorer group - 2 R-2
- Anti-aircraft battery - (4 20 mm cannons)

Initially there were five R-2 wagons in the Regiment's possession at the beginning of February 1945, but when the Soviets arrived at the front, they seized three of them, leaving only two in the Regiment's charge.

On 16 February 1945, when it reached the area of operations, *Regimentul 2 Care de Luptă* had a staff of 1,000 officers, non-commissioned officers and soldiers, equipped with 78 armoured and armoured vehicles. The situation of the Regiment in February 1945 was considered unsatisfactory in numerous aspects, the main ones being:

- shortage of officers and troops was 40 per cent
- insufficient equipment and clothing
- incomplete training
- absence of war experience
- numerical and technical inferiority of tanks and armoured vehicles.

Despite its shortcomings, absences and technical difficulties, *Regimentul 2 Care de Luptă,* from March subordinated to the 27[a] Tank Brigade of the 7th[a] Army of the Soviet Guard, fought in Czechoslovakia and Austria, returning to Czechoslovakia until May 1945. The Regiment was involved in the operations to cross the Hron River where, during the hard fighting that took place between 26 and 27 March, 8 R-35/Vanatorul R-35 tanks were destroyed and two were damaged, and the Nitra and Váh rivers, as well as a series of operations in the mountains, always collaborating with the units of the 27[a] Guard Tank Brigade. *Regimentul 2 Care de Luptă* also participated in the liberation of Bratislava, where it entered the city on 4 April.

Continuing the offensive, the Regiment participated in the crossing of the Morava River on 9 April, entering Austrian territory together with the 27th Soviet Tank Brigade. As of this date, the two R-2s of the Tank Exploring Group were no longer operational, although the reason for this absence is unclear: destroyed by the enemy or irrecoverable failure? There was no field workshop in the regiment, and the distance from Romania prevented the supply of spare parts and supplies, so any damaged or broken-down vehicles were to be considered lost. It should be noted that during the entire operational cycle, the only vehicles that arrived as replacements were three T-4 tanks captured from the Germans, one from the Soviets and two from the Romanian tank drivers.

---

35 The operational activity of AB-Sd.Kfz. 222 continued even after the IIGM, in fact, as of 15 November 1947, the Romanian army still had 13 of them in its possession.

36 At the end of the conflict, there were three SPW-Sd.Kfz. 250 in service.

37 Although no T.As. T3-Stug. III made it to the end of the conflict, by 1947 there were 31 T.As. assault guns in service, including a few T.As. T4-Jagdpanzer IV. These fighters came from the Red Army, which had captured numerous of them, and from the repair of vehicles left on the battlefields. The T.As. T3. remained in service in the Romanian army until 1950, being decommissioned in 1954.

The contribution of *Regimentul 2 Care de Luptă* during the liberation of Austria was crucial in the battles in the districts of Hohenruppersdorf and Schrick. In particular, in the battle to conquer the town of Hohenruppersdorf between 11 and 13 April 1945, the Romanian tank drivers distinguished themselves by facing a series of difficulties they had never before encountered, among others:
- the surprise attack at dawn on the 11th without artillery preparation
- the attack by the enemy air force on 11 and 12
- the tank fighting on day 12, the only incident with the highest tank participation on the Romanian side during the war against German troops.

Further violent fighting saw the Regiment involved, between 14 and 15 April, in the capture of the town of Schrick and in Eisenstadt, where the offensive ended on 20 April 1945. For its active participation in the operations, *Regimentul 2 Care de Luptă* was mentioned in four Soviet agendas issued in the week of 11 to 16 April 1945. On 22 April it began the transfer to Czechoslovakia with its few remaining operational means, among them there were still five T-38 tanks and two TACAM R-2s, but the T-38s were seized by the Soviets.

Due to heavy losses in men and vehicles, *Regimentul 2 Care de Luptă* was contracted to a tank company, which took the name *Duceag Company* after Captain Arcadie Duceag, who took command, always subordinate to the 27[a] Guard Tank Brigade.

The Duceag Company consisted of the following units:
- T-4 tank platoon
- truck platoon and a T.A.C.A.M. R-2[38]
- R-35 Tank Platoon/Vanatorul de Care R-35[39]
- R-1 platoon[40]

The Duceag Company was again involved in hard fighting with the Germans in the last days of April, repelling a number of enemy counter-attacks carried out due to its greater knowledge of the terrain and greater firepower. On 5 May 1945, near the village of Pasohlávky, it sustained its last combat repelling a German counter-attack, losing a TACAM R-2, a Vanatorul de Care R-35 and a T-4 in the encounter.

On 9 May 1945, the survivors of *Regimentul 2 Care de Luptă were* concentrated in the town of Znojmo, near Brno, ready to return to Romania. On that date six tanks were still in service, but only two were operational, from the initial 78 with which the Regiment had begun its participation in the liberation of Czechoslovakia and Austria 45 days earlier!

Thus ended, on foreign soil, the war of the Romanian tank drivers that had begun in June 1941 with the conquest of Bessarabia and Bukovina, almost four years of war in which the valour of the tank drivers sent to fight with obsolete means or not up to those of the enemy had emerged. It was only in 1944, with the entry into service of a few dozen German and national tanks, that the comparison with the enemy's means was more balanced, but the small number of tanks, the lack of spare parts, of field workshops, and the scarce industrialisation, which did not allow the mass production of a few interesting prototypes, never allowed the Romanian armoured units to effectively counter the numerous and well-armed Soviet and, after the armistice, German armoured units.

---

38 Only one TACAM R-2 survived the conflict and is now on display at the National Museum in Bucharest.

39 The last R-35/Vanatorul de Care R-35s were only decommissioned after the end of the IIGM, when armoured vehicles supplied by the Soviet Union arrived.

40 Following the armistice, all 11 R-1 tankettes still in service in the Cavalry were recovered, restored and used in the defence of Bucharest and Ploiești, and then participated in the liberation of Transylvania and then in the war in Czechoslovakia and Austria. They seem to have remained in service until 1955.

▲ Vânători de munte on board an SPW medi during the liberation of Transylvania in September 1944 (*https://it.wikipedia. org/wiki/Vânători_de_munte*)

▼ A T-4 tank belonging to *Regimentul 2 Care de Luptă* during the liberation of Czechoslovakia in the spring of 1945, one can see the white circle with the red star in the centre used after the armistice in 1944 (*http://tankfront.ru/romania/photo. html#!prettyPhoto*)

▲ A Romanian T-4 tank prepares to cross a river, on a floating pontoon launched by Soviet engineers, in April 1945 in Czechoslovakia *(http://wio.ru/tank/romania.htm)*

▼ A T.As. assault cannon. T3 assault gun belonging to the *Regimentul 2 Care de Luptă* engaged in the fighting for the liberation of Czechoslovakia in 1945 *(https://477768.livejournal.com/tag/Румыния)*

▲ Two T.As. assault guns. T3 assault guns, damaged during the fighting for the liberation of Czechoslovakia, loaded onto railway platforms to be sent to workshops in Romania for repairs in 1945 *(https://477768.livejournal.com/tag/Румыния)*

▼ A TACAM T-60 follows a Hungarian 43M Zrínyi II assault gun, captured and re-used by the Romanians, on 14 October 1944 in Dej, during the fighting against Hungarian and German units for the liberation of Transylvania *(https://thearmo-redpatrol.com/2018/08/18/romanian-tanks-in-detail-tacam-t-60-t-60a/)*

▲ Poor quality photograph of a TACAM R-2 with its crew in spring 1944 *(www.facebook.com/Count-High-School-Girls-und-Panzer-1548083418836988)*

▼ The only TACAM R-2 surviving the war and now on display at the Muzeul Militar Naţional 'Regele Ferdinand I' in Bucharest *(https://en.wikipedia.org/wiki/National_Military_Museum,_Romania)*

▲ The TACAM R-2 number plate U-039247 just completed and ready for delivery *(www.youtube.com/watch?v=u8Mt1U-X6uyU)*

▼ A Vânătorul de Care R-35 tank, with the turret turned to 6 o'clock, at Znojmo station in May 1945, note the new badge in force after the 1944 armistice with the white circle and red star in the centre *(https://tanks-encyclopedia.com/ww2/romania/vanatorul-de-care-r35/)*

▲ A Romanian soldier on board a Vânătorul de Care R-35 tank at Znojmo station in May 1945 (*https://tanks-encyclopedia.com/ww2/romania/vanatorul-de-care-r35/*)

▼ A Vânătorul de Care R-35 tank abandoned at Znojmo station in May 1945 amidst destroyed German tanks (*https://tanks-encyclopedia.com/ww2/romania/vanatorul-de-care-r35/*)

▲ Another Vânătorul de Care R-35 tank abandoned at Znojmo station in May 1945 (*https://tanks-encyclopedia.com/ww2/romania/vanatorul-de-care-r35/*)

▲ Vânători de munte posing on a T-38 tank belonging to the *Batalionul care da lupta T-38 in* the summer of 1943 in Crimea *(from: Armata română și evoluția armei tancuri. Documente (1919-1945)- op. cit. in bibliography)*

▲ Michael I cross with white borders painted on the sides of the tank hull *(https://thearmoredpatrol.com/2016/03/20/romanian-tank-destroyers-in-world-of-tanks)*

▲ In this photograph, A TACAM R-2 on display at the National Military Museum, Bucharest. This tank destroyer was built by removing the turret of the R-2 light tank and building a pedestal to mount an ex-Soviet 76.2 mm (3.00 in) ZiS-3 field gun in its place. A three-sided fighting compartment was built to protect the gun and its crew. Twenty were built in 1944. Wikipedia by Mircea 87

▼ A rear view of the Romanian TACAM R-2 tank destroyer. Wikipedia by Lupishor

CAMOUFLAGE, INSIGNIA, REGISTRATION NUMBER

The first armoured cars used by the Romanians in World War I were painted light grey, while those captured were left in their original colour. Tanks purchased after the war were usually left in the original colour in which they left the factory, i.e. dark green for the French R-35s and FT-17s, olive green for the Czechoslovak R-1s and R-2s, panzer grey for the T-38s, although some were in dark yellow (dunkelgelb), panzer grey initially, and then dark yellow for the T-3s, T-4s and T.As. The TACAM T-60s and TACAM R-2s were painted olive green, as were the Malaxa UEs.

Normally the tanks were not camouflaged, only a few T-38s were delivered in dark yellow with thin olive green and brick red streaks, while some second-hand T-4s were in dark yellow with olive green spots. There is photographic evidence of R-35s with typical French camouflage; these may have been Polish tanks confiscated after the surrender of Poland following the German invasion. Some R-35 tanks, during the early stages of the conflict, had painted a blue stripe around the turret.

All Romanian armoured vehicles, until 1940, had the coat of arms of King Carol II painted on the sides of the turret in black, later replaced by the Cross of Michael I (Crucea Mihai I) painted on the sides of the hull. It was painted with white borders if the wagon was dark in colour, or with black borders if the colour of the wagon was light.

As for the aerial recognition of the vehicle, both the Michael I Cross painted, normally in colour or white, on the bonnet of the tanks and a tricolour cockade, in the blue-yellow-red colours of the Romanian flag, were used. On the R-1 tanks, belonging to the Cavalry, the tricolour cockade was painted on the sides of the casemate and on the front bonnet, while on the turret St George slaying the dragon was painted in white.

After the armistice, the tanks belonging to *Regimentul 2 Care de Luptă* were painted a white circle with a red star in the centre on the sides of the turret.

There were no divisional symbols on any medium.

On the tanks belonging to the *Divizia 1 Blindată* were initially painted three-digit numbers on the sides of the turret, in white or black, probably following the German tank numbering scheme, after 1943 this numbering system disappeared and the tanks remained without any numbers. Some second hand T-4s, delivered by the Germans in 1944, retained the original numbering in place in the Wehrmacht.

On R-1, R-2, R-35, Vanatorul de Care R-35, TACAM T-60, Chenillette Malaxa tanks, there was a plate painted in white or black, with a U followed by 6 numbers. It was normally painted on the front wing and rear plate of the tank. On T-3, T-4 and T.As. tanks the plate rarely appears, although it is present in some photographs. On R-1 tankettes the number plate was white with numbers in black painted on the front and rear of the vehicle.

▲ Cross of Michael I painted in colour for aerial identification on the bonnet of tanks, could also be painted white only *(https://thearmoredpatrol.com/2016/03/20/romanian-tank-destroyers-in-world-of-tanks)*

▼ Tricolour air identification cockade painted on R-1 cavalry light tanks, it was also painted on the sides of the casemate *(https://thearmoredpatrol.com/2016/03/20/romanian-tank-destroyers-in-world-of-tanks)*

▲ The white circle with the red star in the centre painted on the sides of the turret on the tanks after the armistice of August 1944 *(https://thearmoredpatrol.com/2016/03/20/romanian-tank-destroyers-in-world-of-tanks)*

▼ On R-1 light wagons in cavalry service, St. George killing the dragon in white was painted on the sides of the turret *(https://thearmoredpatrol.com/2016/03/20/romanian-tank-destroyers-in-world-of-tanks)*

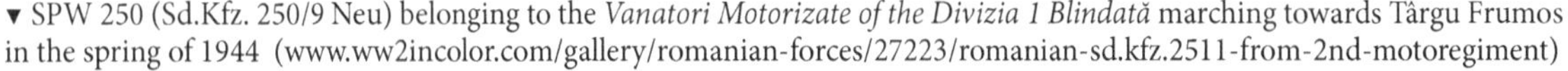

▲ In this photograph, unfortunately of poor quality, a T-4 tank damaged during the war against the Germans in Czecho-slovakia in 1945 can be seen *(www.cartula.ro/forum/topic/2628-panzer-iv-ausf-f2-romanesc/)*

▼ SPW 250 (Sd.Kfz. 250/9 Neu) belonging to the *Vanatori Motorizate of the Divizia 1 Blindată* marching towards Târgu Frumos in the spring of 1944 (www.ww2incolor.com/gallery/romanian-forces/27223/romanian-sd.kfz.2511-from-2nd-motoregiment)

▲ T-4 tanks parade in Bucharest in late 1945, note the crown, symbol of the monarchy, painted on the turret sides and front *(www.cartula.ro/forum/topic/2628-panzer-iv-ausf-f2-romanesc/)*

▼ Section of Renault and Peugeot model 1915 armored cars, belonging to the *Grup de autoblindate*, at the front in 1917 *(www.facebook.com/photo/?fbid=141815861658121&set=pcb.141816238324750*

BIBLIOGRAPHY

Books

- AA.VV., "Armata Romana 1941 – 1945", RAI, 1996.
- AA.VV., "Armata română şi evoluţia armei tancuri. Documente (1919-1945)", Editura Universităţii din Piteşti, 2012.
- Axworthy M., Serbanescu H., "The Romanian Army of World War "", Osprey Military n. 246.
- Dumitru I. S."Tancuri În Flăcări", Editura Nemira, 1999.
- Halbac N., "Scurt istoric al Armei Tancuri", s.i.d.

Websites

- https://thearmoredpatrol.com/2016/03/20/romanian-tank-destroyers-in-world-of-tanks/
- http://ftr-wot.blogspot.com/2013/05/romanian-armor-part-i-pre-ww2.html
- http://wio.ru/tank/romania.htm
- http://it.topwar.ru
- http://tankfront.ru
- https://tanks-encyclopedia.com/ww2/romanian-tanks-ww2.php
- www.worldwar2.ro/media/?article=366
- www.flamesofwar.com/hobby.aspx?art_id=1021
- https://gmic.co.uk/blogs/entry/532-romanian-armoured-vehicles-used-betwen-1919-1947/
- https://thereaderwiki.com/en/Romanian_armored_fighting_vehicle_production_during_World_War_II
- www.rumaniamilitary.ro/istoria-artileriei-romane-autotunurile#prettyPhoto
- www.zimmerit.com/zimmeritpedia/ROMANIA_sez_1.html
- www.eurasia1945.com/batallas/contienda/asedio-de-odessa/
- http://enciclopediaromaniei.ro/wiki/Trupele_blindate
- www.worldwar2.ro/media/?article=366
- www.istoria.md/articol/822/Luptele_trupelor_blindate_din_Armata_Romana_in_Bucovina,_Basarabia,_Ucraina_si_Crimeea
- http://stiintele-educatiei.myforum.ro/file-dintr-un-jurnal-de-front-1941-vt260.html
- https://forum.axishistory.com/viewtopic.php?t=197798
- https://forums.tripwireinteractive.com/index.php?threads/the-siege-of-odessa.8416/
- https://daydaynews.cc/en/military/605814.html
- www.semperfidelis.ro/e107_plugins/forum/forum_viewtopic.php?43741.135
- https://gaz.wiki/wiki/it/Romania_in_World_War_II
- www.redescoperaistoria.ro/2013/10/16/tancul-lupta-cu-pumnul-de-fier-3/

TITOLI GIÀ PUBBLICATI - TITLES ALREADY PUBLISHING

BOOKS TO COLLECT